Genealogical Abstracts

of

Edgefield
South Carolina

Equity Court
Records

Carol Wells

HERITAGE BOOKS
2010

HERITAGE BOOKS
AN IMPRINT OF HERITAGE BOOKS, INC.

Books, CDs, and more—Worldwide

For our listing of thousands of titles see our website
at
www.HeritageBooks.com

Published 2010 by
HERITAGE BOOKS, INC.
Publishing Division
100 Railroad Ave. #104
Westminster, Maryland 21157

International Standard Book Numbers
Paperbound: 978-0-7884-2100-6
Clothbound: 978-0-7884-8529-9

FOREWORD

Equity Court records are a rich source of genealogical facts. In the course of settling disputed or complicated inheritances, names of stepchildren, half siblings, maiden names, deceased husbands, first, second, third spouses, extended family relations may all be part of testimony. Suits for separate maintenance show the deplorable situation of women when married to violent or unstable husbands. Here we find families torn by dissention, abused wives, dishonest guardians, contentious relatives, and at least one destroyed will. Other official records and family bibles cannot compare with the revelation of troubles and relationships found in Equity Court holdings.

In many suits dozens of pieces of evidence have been compressed into a few paragraphs of names, dates, situation, and decree. Not every case is complete. The old petitions, evidence, financial accounts, replies are discolored, torn, bled through, fragmented, blotted, or illegible. In all cases, original documents should be viewed.

These abstracts were made from microfilm. All names are printed to the best of my ability to read them, often appearing in several spellings. There are also troubles of doubtful words where certain letters can appear similar in careless handwriting [Is the name Hitt or Hill?]. All names and places are indexed. Although one suit concerns a transaction made in 1736, most problems fall between 1790 and 1820.   Carol Wells

Abbreviations

dmr	administrator
fsd	aforesaid
gt	against
CEED	Commissioner Edgefield Equity District
lk	clerk
omplts	complainants
omr	commissioner
au	daughter
ec, decd	deceased
D.S.	Deputy Surveyor
Exr, exor	executor
lleg	illegible
lff	plaintiff
ec	recorded
i l	son in law
ol	solicitor
wp	township
vill	last will and testament
vit	witness

Equity. "The pursuit of fairness....A body of law that seeks to achieve fairness on an individual basis....Equity is contrary to the notion that law is simply the strict, formal interpretation of statutes and precedent.... Equity decisions cannot be decided by a jury and are left to the sound discretion of a judge." Wests Encyclopedia of American Law, Vol. 4, pages 290, 291.

United States Constitution. Article III, Sec 2, Clause 1, "judicial Power shall extend to all Cases, in Law and Equity."

GENEALOGICAL ABSTRACT OF EDGEFIELD EQUITY COURT RECORDS

FILM #JR 4067 Original bills and cross bills. Files 1-3 containing 401 items.
    Jacob Zinn Jr & his wife Mary vs John Ardis, Giles Bowers, David Bowers
9 November 1816. To Walter Leigh, John Miller, James S Walker and William Micou Esqrs.
Testimony of Richmond County, GA, persons needed. Whitfield Brooks commissioner in
Equity. Judges Henry William Desaussure, Theodore Gaillard, Thomas Waties, William
James, Waddy Thompson. Jacob Zinn the elder, apptd guardian of John Ardis, a minor, in
Spring 1813. Isaac Ardis of Beach Island, Edgefield District, died intestate May or June 1795
leaving widow Mary Ardis and sd John Ardis heir and only child. Jacob Zinn appointed
guardian by Court of Ordinary in the spring of 1813. On 5 January 1796 David Ardis
administered on estate of Isaac Ardis, Abraham Ardis and Alexander Downer securities,
returned inventory and appraisement of personal estate 27 February 1796. Sale 4 April 1796
of some personal property. On July 4, 1796 returned by administrator David Ardis; account
current made by Cradock Burnell made after death of sd David Ardis on 27 October 1801.
Cradock Burnell and Abraham Ardis executors of will of David Ardis. On 27 May 1800
Jacob Zinn the younger took out letters of administration on sd estate. Jacob Zinn the younger
took possession of three fifths of the lands which sd Isaac decd possessed and has constantly
planted. Sd Isaac derived his title to lands from his father Mathias Ardis who died in Sa-
annah in 1781 or 1782; his will devised all his real estate to his wife Christian Ardis during
her life after which to be divided amongst his children, viz David youngest, Daniel next and
successively to Abraham, Sarah, Joseph, Isaac, John and Elizabeth. Mary Ardis eldest child
excluded. John, Elizabeth, and Jacob died before their Mother and Daniel after, but before
he was of age and before said devisees came into possession of their land which contained by
the original grant 300 acres but by resurvey 400 acres. Christian Ardis the widow died 6 May
1785. Isaac was in undisturbed possession. Sarah Ardis married Benjamin Bowers, who died
without lawful issue living at time of his death leaving his widow Sarah who on 25 April 1791
conveyed her part by deed to sd Isaac . John's part fell to his sister Elizabeth who married
Francis Carlisle both of whom died without issue before they possessed their part. About four
months after the death of sd Isaac his widow Mary Ardis married James Richards and died
about six weeks after marriage without dower or any part of sd lands having been assigned
to her and her husband. John Ardis, your orators ward, at time of his father's death was only
one or two years old. Nathaniel Howell the elder was appointed his guardian on 6 January
1796 giving bond with George Bender and William Shinholster securities, bond renewed 6
March 1800, John Clark and Casper Nail securities. Surveyor William Minor divided land
into three tracts, giving one to James Richards until 1801; James Richards being deeply in
debt took French leave and (as it is said) retired to Spanish Territory. Judgment agt Samuel
Devall on a note; note agt John Prior, note agt John Sturzenegger which notes were never
collected for 10 or 12 years after they became due and must be charged to Nathaniel Howell
former guardian. Your orator has received no monies or property belonging to sd minor except
S Devalls debt. Certification 28 April 1813 by Jno Simkins CED. Summons to Cradock
Burnell, Abram Ardis, Simeon Cushman served 14 May 1817 by Sheriff J Hatcher. 1816
summons to Benjamin Hightower, John Tarrance, James Hunter and John Clarke Esquires to
examine witnesses. Bill of exceptions mentions notes: Saml Duval, Joseph Butler, Wm
Butler, John J Tobler, Jno Sturzenegger; Jno Prior, Alexr Downer; Howell & Parker;
Shinholster; signed by Chris Goodwin, Edmund Bacon for dfts. Will of Christian Ardis, 7
October 1783; /s/ Chris (x) Ardis. Wit Cradk Burnell, Thomas Rogers. Rec 1795 Richd Tutt

Clk. Affidavit of Jacob Zinn that his defence has been delayed by death of his two year old child and sickness of others, 1 October 1815.

John Ardis vs Cradock Burnell and others, 6 June 1815, to Charles Goodwin solicitor for Jacob Zinn and Nathl Howell signed Simkins & McDuffie plffs sol. Georgia: to Superior Court, Richmond County, Petition of Benjamin Harris. Mary Bowers and Lud Harris admrs estate of Benjamin Bowers decd. Benjn Bowers promissory note to pay John Garrett twenty three pounds fourteen shillings eleven pence by 21 December 1786; Garrett assigned sd note unto petitioner; Seaborn Jones, plff atty. Benjn Harris vs admrs of B Bowers, summons by George Walton Esqr to appear 23 March; Will Robertson clk. Acknowledgment 16 January 1801 by Lud Harris. Certification by Robert Raymond Reid Judge of Superior Court 30 April 1818, that John H Mann is clerk of Superior Court of Richmond County. January 30, 1817 deposition of Alexr Downer. Wit B Hightower, John Tarrance.

John Ardis, James Hunter & John Clark vs Jacob Zinn junr & wife. Precept 10 January 1737; Jas Gillespie D.S. laid off unto Robert McMurdy 300 acres in Granville County, New Windsor Twp adj land of Martha McGillvery, Robert Vaughan, Savannah River; signed 2 May 1738; Columbia, certified true copy by Jesse Kilgore 2 Feby 1816.

Archd McKoy(McCoy) attended, distance of 100 miles, 7 Feby 1818. Oath of John Ardis that conveyance deed from Sarah Bowers to his father Isaac Ardis is not in his possession, 4 Feby 1818; further, that Nathaniel Howell informed him that it was lost or mislaid.

Account of sales of property of Isaac Ardis, 4 April 1796. Sales to James Richards, David Ardis, Stephen Randolph, Jonathan Meyer, Lemuel Young, John Pryor, William Williams, Walter Taylor, Abram Ardis, Nathaniel Howell, Doctor Dysart, Jacob Gaylon, Alexander Downer, Joseph Cox, Jacob Zinn, Nathaniel Howell, Benjamin Noland, Henry Turkenet, Miles Livinsworth, Thomas Rogers, William Shinholster, Wm Parker, Harrison Bell.

Nathaniel Howell ads John Ardis. Summons to John Prior, John Star, John Sturzenegger, 4 January 1816 as witnesses.

Jacob Zinn Junr and Mary his wife only child of Benjamin Bowers & Sarah his wife, agt John Ardis, David Bowers Jr, Giles Bowers, executors of David Bowers decd, Isaac Ardis and David Bowers Senr were exors of Ben Bowers decd. Cross Bill. Jane Fuller, witness. Grant by Wm Bull Lt Governor to Robert McMurdy, 300 acres in New Windsor Twp in Granville County adj Martha McGilvery, Robert Vaughan, Savannah River, 12 September 1741.

Cradock Burnell vs Peter Lamkin and Caspar Nail, 28 Oct 1819. Bill of Sale, 3 May 1791. John Diampert of Columbia, Georgia, sold to Isaac Ardis of Edgefield Negroes Jemima, Abbey, and Will; wit Cradock Burnell, Jacob Zinn Jr.

John Ardis now of age lately by his guardian Jacob Zinn vs Cradock Burnell, Abraham Ardis, Jacob Zinn Junr, Nathaniel Howell, Ann Howell, Jonathan Philips, Elbert Philips, William Baker, Aaron Barkeley, Archibald McCoy, Hartwell Howell, Casper Howell, Abram Baker,

GENEALOGICAL ABSTRACT OF EDGEFIELD EQUITY COURT RECORDS

3 June 1815, Whit Brooks. Examinations of Sophia Harris, Sarah Pardieu & Henry Zinn to be taken in Georgia, also Major Jacob Zinn, Alexander Downer, & Jane Fuller, also Craddock Burnell, Harden Blalock, John Star, and Simeon Cushman.

Deposition of Alexander Downer 25 January 1817; wit B Hightower, Jas Hunter, John Tarrance. Deposition of Sarah Pardieu. Benjamin Bowers purchased shares of Francis & Elisabeth Carlile. They were entitled to one share of land in their own right and two Negroes Duomony and Abbey and on right of John Ardis of one share of land and one Negro named Will. Land of Mathias Ardis was willed to eight legatees; believes Isaac Ardis clear of debt at time of his death; /s/ Sarah (x) Pardieu. Certified by W Micou, Walter Leigh. Deposition of Sophia Harris: was acquainted with Mathias Ardis and Christian his wife; daughter Elisabeth married a Carlile. /s/ Sophia Harris. 28 Dec 1816. Wm Micou, Walter Leigh.

Will of Mathias Ardis Senr of New Windsor Twp, 29 October 1774: to dau Mary Negro Charles; to son Mathew Negro girl Rose and her issue; to daughter Elizabeth Negroes Quomoni and Sally; to son Isaac two Negroes Dick and Sue; to son Jacob Negro Dina & her issue; to dau Sarah two Negroes Jack and Rodger; to son Abraham Negro Jimmy, to son Daniel two Negroes Boatswain and Harry; to son David two Negroes Mall [Mabl?] and Judy and their issue; my land in whatever place unto my eight younger children to be equally divided amongst them; if it should happen that my son David should die before he receives his legacy then his legacy to fall to Daniel; if Daniel should die before he receives his part then that part to Abraham, and so on successively, the ninth being Mary the eldest child. No legatee to receive any part until decease of Christian my wife to whom I bequeath all and every part. /s/ Mathias Ardis. Wit James Thompson, John Beddingfield, Ninian[?] Patric.

Deposition of Alexander Downer taken 25 Jan 1817. I lived in the house with her & her sons about the year 1783 and ever since lived within one mile & a half of the sd Plantation. I do not know whether he gave his Brother any part or not. /s/ Alex Downer. Wit B Hightower, Jas Hunter, John Tarrance.

Deposition of Lud Harris, Richmond Co, Ga, 3 October 1817; was admr estate of Benjamin Bowers in Richmond County, estate indebted to Benjamin Harris; was sued as admr of sd estate by Benjamin Harris and he recovered judgment. I never was guardian of Mary Zinn but I was conversant with affairs of her father's estate, a debt charged in account of Isaac Ardis agt estate of Benjm Bowers paid by sale of land afsd; also that Patrick Hays presented an account on estate of B Bowers.

Summons issued 13 May 1817 to John Mathews, Morlow L Prior, James Russeau, William Sandford, Frederick Sandford Esquires or any two of them. Summons to Briton Mims, Hezekiah Dickinson, John H Mann

FILM # JR 4068 Equity Records, Files Numbers 1, 2, and 3.

John Ryan Esq exr of Benj Ryan &devisees on his will vs Samuel Marsh, Milly his wife, extx of Benj Ryan & Mary Johnson extx of Richd Johnson. Partition. From uncommon high spirit of decd Milly Marsh and her control over estate of Benjamin Ryan especially money in specie which he had long hoarded, complainants believe she never permitted Samuel Marsh to have control over same. In 1815 when Samuel Marsh applied to her for pocket money for his eldest son Samuel Marsh, then a student at Columbia College, she refused in acrimonious terms. Milly never intended Samuel Marsh to have control of property bequeathed to her by her deceased husband; she entered marriage contract with Samuel Marsh previous to marriage. All has fallen to Samuel Marsh and not to complainants. He has not only executed acts of ownership but has removed furniture, has placed Thomas Marsh in the dwelling house who hath several negroes, Old Ned, Amy, and Rachel, tending about ten acres of cotton which Milly Marsh planted independent of plantation in care of Jesse Bettis. Complainant John Ryan applied to Samuel Marsh not to interfere. Complainant fears estate will be wasted if proceeds of crops go to Samuel Marsh or if Jesse Bettis or Thomas Marsh should give him possession of sd premises. When Benjamin Ryan died he had a large sum of money in specie that remained in possession of Milly Marsh. Samuel Marsh possessed himself of same. Samuel Marsh was anxious shortly after she was shot to get two keys out of her pocket to open a desk in the chamber of the house in which she was murdered. Coroner gave him the keys after inquest on the body. At least five hundred dollars was taken. Milly departed this life on 29th May last by which melancholy event management of estate of deceased Benjamin Ryan hath devolved on complainant John Ryan Sr. By his will, his personal estate should be divided as therein expressed between his wife and the children of his sd nephew and niece complainants as afsd, with the exception of three negroes to be freed at her death before any division takes place. Milly Marsh died without having had opportunity of pointing out to whom she meant to give her share of the personal property under sd will. Complainant John Ryan Sr charges that Milly Marsh never expressed to him as exr any desire for division of personal property. He believes Samuel Marsh in virtue of his marital rights hath taken out lettersadmn on her estate as having died intestate, Allen B Addison and Abner Blocker, securities, to exclusion of her next of kin. Millie Marsh had only a life estate in the real property of her first husband; on her death the use of same absolutely vested in the other devisees in sd will, nephew Benjamin Ryan and S Galman . Samuel Marsh and wife Milly at beginning of present year hired overseer Jesse Bettis, placed him on the plantation of the estate with twenty one Negroes belonging to same: Charles, Gibb, Isaac, Jack, David, Cato, Pulaski, Ben, Jere, Peter, Shepherd, Young Ned, Silvy, Cate, Jas, Harriet, Mary, Connetta, Clara, Hannah, and Milly. Jesse Bettis produced eighty acres cotton, 200 acres corn. Complainant asks that Samuel Marsh, Jesse Bettis, Thomas Marsh, John Lolly, and Mary Johnson make answers upon oath. Goodwin & Bacon, complainants sol. 30 Sept 1816.

Mrs Mary Johnson extx of Richard Johnson decd. Her deceased husband an exr of will of Benjamin Ryan Sr. She denies her husband took any property or profits thereof, believes part of property was sold by court order, 2 October 1816; /s/ Mary (x) Johnson.

Judge Desaussure ordered monies belong to the wife. Part of property sold, only part of money received, exr Rd Johnson indebted to estate. Note of Barkley Ferguson & John Hardy. Accounts 1 January 1817. Sales to Jeremiah Hatcher, Benjamin Gallman, Starling Mitchell, John Grice, Mrs Jones.

Answer of Samuel Marsh. Amelia Ryan, came into possession of estate; Marsh married Amelia in 1815, assumed administration as exr in right of his wife, judgment obtained by Jacob Stott agt Benjamin Ryan Sr and wife for an assault committed by the then Mrs Ryan; during pendency of appeal Benjamin Ryan died; dft married his widow. When appeal was determined execution was issued and part of lands of estate was levied on by sheriff without knowledge of dft, sold at public outcry, purchased by Allen B Addison for this dft. One hundred sixty Dollars was all the money in the house at his wife's death except a small sum his wife had made by selling butter. His wife being displeased at reports abroad about the marriage contract, requested that it be destroyed, which was done by mutual consent.

Abraham Odum vs Saml Marsh. Odum testifies that Theophilus Williams is son of Mary Williams, sister to Milley Marsh; his parents are dead. Mary Williams left three children: Theophilus and two dau. Martha Williams is sister to Theophilus Williams & living with him.

Martha Williams states Mary Odom married Sampson Williams, father of Theophilus. Mrs Williams had three children: James, Patty, and Theophilus. Mrs. Williams did not remarry, lived with man named Parish, had no children by him. He left her. Mary Williams and huband both dead; knows Theophilus is son of Mary Williams.

Jacob Odom states he is acquainted with Celia Boatwright who is the daughter of Lewis Odom who was the brother of Milly Marsh. Lewis Odom had only two children, Celia and Lewis. Lewis left this country, not heard of since, believes him to be dead.

Richard Newman states he often has seen Abraham Odom at Mrs Marshes and they acknowledged being brother and sister. He is dead, was told so by A Odom one of the sons of the decd. A Odom's children are scattered through the world.

Theo Williams testifies that Martha Williams, sister, is dau of Mary Williams Decd who was sister of whole blood to Milly Marsh. Mary had only three children. Abraham Odom Jr of Barnwell is son of Abraham Odum decd, brother of Milly Marsh.

Mr Richard Newman swears Willis Odum and Milly Marsh are brother and sister. Willis Odum as brother of the whole blood is a claimant of part of Milly Marsh's estate.

Wilson Barrenton says about twenty years ago he saw Willis Odum and believes present claimant to be same man, that he is brother of whole blood to Milly Marsh.

Theophilus Williams testifies that Jane Huddleston is daughter of Mary Williams who was the sister of Milley Marsh and full sister to himself, that his mother had only three children, Jane, Patty & himself. That his sister Jane married Joseph Huddleston.

John Mitchell testifies that Nancy Craven[?] is only child living of Jacob Odom who was brother of whole blood to Milly Marsh.

John Ryan exr vs Saml Marsh & others. Richard Newman & wife et al vs Saml Marsh & others. Decree in these cases: estate is to be divided equally between representatives of Benj Ryan and Samuel Marsh & the half decreed to Saml Marsh to be divided between sd Marsh and the reps of Milley Marsh his wife who are eight in number. Share of Jno Ryan, of Benj Ryan, of Benj Gallman. 6 Jany 1821; Whit Brooks.

Same vs Same. Relationship to Milley Marsh of persons claiming shares of her estate. Theophilus Williams. Sarah Beasly, Marlborough Dist. Willis Odum. Martha Williams dau of Martha Odom Williams. Children of Abraham Odom decd.

Deed, John Ryan to Benjamin Ryan, 75 acres adj lines of Benjamin Ryan Senr, Saml Walker. 17 August 1811, NB 15l acres were conveyed by Lacon Ryan to Jacob Clevling and by Jacob Clevling to Benjamin Ryan and John Ryan and I make my title to one half of above. /s/ John Ryan. Wit Capt Richard Johnson, James Lamar, William Nobles. Proven 5 May 1815 by Johnson; M Mims CCP.

Letter of Attorney, Benjamin Odom of Morgan County, Georgia, to John P Odom of Walton County, Georgia, to recover my interest in estate of Emillia Ryan decd which I am entitled to in right of my father Abram Odom brother to sd Emilia Ryan decd. 2 June 1823 /s/ Benjamin Ryan. Wit John M Cox JP. J[?] Cannon[?]

Sales of Benj Ryan's estate 1 January 1819. to Reuben Cloud, John Harbuck, Thos Christian, John Cobb, Starling Mitchel, Sarah Harden, Jas Parker, Mrs Nobles, Mary Johnson, Thos Marsh, Dr R Reid, Geo Butler Esq, Mrs Numan, Gasper Donaldson, Eli Morgan, Dennis Carpenter, John Ryan Senr, John Doby, Samp Butler, Wilson Whatley, Jesse Blocker, Jas Scott, Jas Beavins, Edmd Bugg, A B Addison, Thomas Marsh, John E Ryan, Benj Runnell, Edward Jones, Isaac Randolph, David Donaldson. To Saml Marsh Negro woman Amy & children Mary and Bob, boys Lonijo and Nero, woman Kate & children Clary & Maria, Peter, Ben, girl Becky and boy Moses, fellow Charles. To Benjamin Gallman Clary & children Milley and Sally, boy Shepherd, boy Alfred, fellow Isaac, woman Mary. To Jno Johnson fellow Jack. To John Ryan Old Ned, boy Jerry, girl Harriett & children Green and Mahala. To Revd Saml Marsh Negro man Dave, Little Ned, Altama, Milley, Silvy and children Henry and William. To Saml Quarles Rachel and two young children, boy Richard. To Benjamin Gallman Sue & her child, Moses, Thursa (small girl) 75 acres, girl Hannah.

Estate of Benjamin Ryan decd, Saml Marsh exr. Paid William Smith, Eldred Simkins, Benjn Ryan, Robert Stark, Josiah Allen, Wm Ellison, John Kerry, Bailey Marshal, John Campbell, Moses Scott, John Ryan, Wm Hill, John Henncy, Wm Hudle, Stephen Tillman, James Butler, Francis Bettis, Thos Marsh, Ab Blocker, Jery Scott, Moses Scott, Whitfield Brooks, John Grice. Received from Richard Johnson, Frances Lamar, Dennis Carpenter, Edwd Johns, Enorah Felps, John Gray, Thomas Carvey, John Hardy, Barkley Fargeson ballance on Negro Cato, Jamy Cleveling. Sworn 23 May 1817.

Administrators bond of Samuel Marsh, Robert Marsh and Jesse Blocker unto John Ryan Esqr surviving exr of Benjamin Ryan decd. Wit Whit Brooks, Levin Rarden.

Deed, 30 August 1810, John Ryan to Benjamin Ryan, 20 acres headwaters of Horns Creek being part of 1000 acres originally granted unto sd John Ryon by Gov Thos Pinckney 3 March 1788. /s/ John Ryan. Wit Wm Hill, Wm Smith, Saml Beams. Relinquishment of dower by Martha Ryon wife of John Ryon [date blank]. Proven 17 Feb 1815 by James Beams; M Mims CCP.

Letter of Attorney. Celia Boatright of Marlborough District to John S Glascock to recover portion of estate of Milley Marsh, 19 November 1819 /s/ Celia Boatright. Wit John Brown, Amelia W Carloss.

GENEALOGICAL ABSTRACT OF EDGEFIELD EQUITY COURT RECORDS

Letter 28 Dec 1817 from John Cheney, Augusta, to Chas Goodwin, enclosing execution.

Order of sale 5 May 1814, sale personal property of Benjamin Ryan decd, sold to Richard Johnson, James Lamar, Denny Carpenter, Edmund Jones, James Clicoling, Thomas Harvy, Enoch Phelps, John Gray Senr, James Reynolds. /s/ Richard Johnson exr. Certified 1 Nov 1815 by Jn Simkins OED.

Benjamin Ryan vs Robert Samuel. Simkins for plf and Goodwin &Y J for dft. Case abated by death of plff. Benj Ryan vs John Kenney. Case Abated. M Mims CCP.

Sworn statement of Sarah (x) Besely, Marlborough Dist, 17 Nov 1819, that she knows Celia Boatright to be legitimate daughter of Lewis Odom and his only surviving child. Aaron Pearson JP.

Statement of William Dobey, 23 October 1815 regarding land of Captain Benjamin Ryan on Horns Creek, part cut down by Edward Jones son in law & overseer for Samuel Marsh and the part that was grubbed was done by John Odum also overseer of sd Samuel Marsh, under orders of Samuel Marsh and his wife. Sworn 23 October 1815 before Chas Goodwin, NP.

Mr Geo Parker proves five days attendance, 6 June 1817; M Mims CCP.

List of Negroes hired January 1817. Rachel & 3 children to Ben Ryan, Colyet to A G Nayle, Derry, Ned, Sue & 3 children to Edward Bacon, Polaski to N Fox, Hannah to R Reid, Milly to Jos Allen, Silvia & 2 children to Edward Bacon, Altamont to R C Lewis, Harriet & 3 children, Old Ned, Dave to Edmund Bacon. List of same, 1818. Rachel & 3 children, Milly, Little Ned to A B Addison, Dave, Colyet to James Bilbo, Polaski to E Jones, Sue & 3 chldren to John Farrow, Silvia & 2 children to R Reid, Jerry to Saml Marsh, Old Ned to W Mays, Altamont to A Landrum, Hannah to Dr Reid.

FILM NO. JR. 4068. Equity Records File numbers 4-10.

Mary Martin by her next friend John Robinson vs David Martin. Bill for separate maintenance. Judges Henry William Desaussure, Theodore Gaillard, Waddy Thompson, Thomas Waties, and William D James. Mary married David Martin about 12 March 1807, was used harshly, with merciless cruelty. In June 1808 she left David. She started to return in company with her mother and Mr George Sawyers. David said if she would not take such usage she might go to the devil. In 1814 Mary offered to return to him but he refused to receive her, later agreed if she would submit to cruelties. David owns house, land, three Negroes, &c. Jinkins & McDuffie. /s/ Mary Martin. 11 Feby 1815. Eldred Simkins JQU. David Martin ads Mary Martin. Bill for separate maintenance. Mentions Mary's ungovernable disposition. Only once did she ask to return, & this after she had a child which she acknowledges was child of Foats[?] [last sentence has worn off the page] /s/ Bacon. Sworn 15 May 1816, Whit Brooks. /s/ David Martin.

Mary Martin vs David Martin. Bill for Alimony, June Term 1818. Infidelity of complainant established, it is unnecessary to enquire further as to her claim for alimony. State does not allow divorce. Bill dismissed. 2 June 1818. /s/ W Thompson. Summons to Polly Taylor alias Mary Martin, and David Martin, February 1817. Deposition of Ridgeway Hogans, 2 June 1817, wit for David Martin.

GENEALOGICAL ABSTRACT OF EDGEFIELD EQUITY COURT RECORDS

Tobias Prior & wife Mary vs Rebecca Bittle et al. Petition for part of succession. To David Bowers, Casper Nail Sr, John Burgess, John Clark jr, John Sturzenegger, Esqrs. Tobias Prior's wife Mary formerly Mary Bruner. Michael Bruner died intestate leaving widow Rebecca and children, Sally, Daniel, minors, and Mary Prior late Mary Bruner. Edgefield land 326 acres on road from Augusta to Minors bridge on Hollow Cr, Silver Bluff, includes head of Musterfield branch; 250 acres on Savannah River purchased of Henry Jones; 150 acres on marsh between Beach Island and high land above Hollow cr and Silver Bluff mills; two tracts 123 ½ acres on road to Minors Bridge adj lands of John Dicks, David Meyers, and estate of Allen Nesbit. Tobias and Mary claim 1/3 of 2/3. On motion of John S. Jeter, land to be divided among Rebecca Bittle formerly Rebecca Bruner, Tobias Prior & wife late Mary Bruner, Sally Bruner, and Daniel Bruner. February 1818. Whitfield Brooks.
Return of commissioners 28 May 1818. To Rebecca Bittle 1/3 of tract whereon she now resides and other land, land to Tobias Prior, to Horatio Collins and wife Sally, to Daniel Bruner. /s/ Casper Nail Sr, David Bowers, John Clarke Jr. Undated financial settlements.

Surviving exors of John Prior vs Charles Goodwin, bill to foreclose mortgage. 19 April 1817. John Prior died 179[blank], having appointed John Star, Jacob Zinn, and his son John Prior exrs of his will, to execute titles to James Olid Prentis; Prentis not able to comply with terms surrendered land to exrs who sold to Charles Goodwin for benefit of estate; Goodwin's bond 22 Jany 1802 conditioned for payment. Tract adj lands of John Gray, Nathaniel Howel, Red Horse Tract, heirs of Harmon Bozeman, Thomas Lamar, Isaac Parker, John Butler, Jacob Zinn jr, boundary between Edgefield & Barnwell Districts; another tract the late John Prior bought of David Zubly on Town Creek, 1000 acres adj some land sd John Prior conveyed to James Olis Prentis, land of late Samuel Burgess, land of George Miller. Provided sd Charles Goodwin paid money according to conditions of mortgage. [Reply of Charles Goodwin cannot be read on microfilm]. June Term 1818. Order commissioners sell lands . W Thompson. Bond 22 Jany 1802 signed by Chas Goodwin, LeRoy Hammond, witnesses Charles Ramsey, William Stewart. John Star & Jacob Zinn vs Chas Goodwin. Purchase contract, 23 January 1802. Sarah Prior to W. Brooks her share from sale of Town Creek land, /s/ Sarah Prior, 28 August 1820; witness Stephen Wilson. Receipts signed by Whit Brooks. Stephen Wilson, Sarah Prior, John Burgess.

Richard Newman and Priscilla, Willis Odum, Jane Odum vs Samuel Marsh, partition, filed June 1817. Priscilla Newman is daughter and only surviving child of Sealy Holland formerly Sealy Odum who married with Holland both of whom are now dead. Milly Marsh's brothers and sisters of whole blood: Sealy Holland, Willis Odum, Jane Odum, Abraham Odum died leaving Abraham, Nancy, Vicey, Milly, Lewis, Jancy, Sally, and Benjamin Odum his children, Jacob Odum died leaving one child Nancy, brother Lewis Odum died leaving one child named Sealy; sister Mary Odum who married [blank] Williams (both dead) who left a son Theophilus Williams and two daughters Jane and Patty Williams. Another brother Michael Odum died leaving no legitimate child. Previous to Milly's marriage with Samuel Marsh they entered a marriage contract by which she secured to herself and her relatives all property to which she was then entitled by virtue of her former husband Benjamin Ryan's will, only allowing to Samuel Marsh a maintenance. Marriage contract has been destroyed by Samuel Marsh who now contends for whole of personal and half of estate of Milly Marsh. Milly Marsh died 1816.

8

intestate, leaving considerable estate; heirs entitled to distribution. Heirs: John Ryan, only surviving executor of Captain Benjamin Ryan Sr, deceased, Lacon Ryan, eldest son of Benjamin Ryan Jr, nephew of sd Benjamin Ryan Sr, John Ryan, Benjamin Jabez Ryan, Margaret Ryan, Sampson Ryan, Stanmore B Ryan, Pickens E Ryan and William C Ryan, children of sd nephew Benjamin Ryan Sr, Mary by next friend Benjamin Gallman, otherwise Goldman, and John Elder Moore, Elizabeth Moore, Rachel H Gallman, William G Gallman, Elizabeth S Gallman, Priscilla H Gallman, and Susan H Gallman children of Sarah Gallman lately the widow of George B Moore and formerly Sarah Ryan niece of sd Benjamin Ryan Sr, minors by sd Benjamin Gallman their next friend. Sd Benjamin Ryan Sr was possessed of considerable real and personal estate, left will dated 20 September 1808, a few specific legacies excepted, gave to wife Milly Ryan all my real and personal estate, at her death to be equally divided to children of my nephew Benjamin Ryan Sarah Goldman, otherwise Gallman. Sets certain Negroes free at wife's death: Ned, Yellow Will, Rachel and three children, Celiny, Polashy, Hannah, Milly. Wife extx, friend Richard Johnson and brother John Ryan exrs. Testator died about 11 November 1813. Complainants desire their share according to testator's will. Richard Johnson died in August 1815. Estate being wasted by Samuel Marsh...cut down woodlands, cut down a large cherry tree in the graveyard at his plantation where he was buried and has been the burying ground of Ryan family since they removed to this State. Cato valued at four hundred Dollars part of sd estate. Barkley Ferguson Esqr of Beaufort Dist was largely indebted to testator gave a Negro boy Benjamin in part payment and Cato for balance of debt, gave bill of sale to Samuel Marsh and wife and not to Benjamin Ryans estate. Sold sundry articles listed in bill of appraisement, a bay horse exchanged with Jeremiah Hatcher Esqr [etc]. Samuel Marsh and Milly his wife confederating with Mary Johnson and others to defraud the devisees in sd Testators will and defeat them of the benefit intended. Desires court to subpoena Samuel Marsh, wife Milly, Mary Johnson to answer to complainants. Goodwin & Bacon solicitors. John Ryan sworn [day lost in discoloration] May 1816; /s/ John Ryan.

Answer of Samuel Marsh to complaint of Willis Odum, Jane Odum and others. Estate of Benjamin Ryan dec was much involved in litigation. Marriage contract was destroyed by mutual wish. Principal object of agreement was to keep each estate of contracting parties separate so that one should not be subject to suits in which the other might be involved. He has repeatedly told him that she considered the whole estate his at her death. Simkins & McDuffie dfts sols. 8 Jany 1818. /s/ Saml Marsh

Decree of Court of Appeals in case of R Newman & wife vs Saml Marsh. Court has not said a word about the costs. It has merely reversed the decree of the Circuit Court as to the Negroes. 8 June 1820. Thos T Willisson. Whitfield Brooks Esqr. Dr. Maxzey died on Sunday night last with the most violent attack of the choleri Morbus, a more distressed family I never saw. T T Willisson.

Richard Newman & others vs Saml Marsh et al. Abraham Odom et al vs Saml Marsh et al. Share due to each of the legatees. June term 1819.

Reeves Martin vs Eliza Goode and Susannah Goode, Bill for Partition. Reeves Martin and Mackeness Goode on 4 November 1817 purchased of John Poole 600 acres on Halfway swamp of Saluda River adj land [fold in paper torn] William Summers. Mackerness Goode died 14 Jany 1818 intestate leaving widow Eliza Goode and child Susannah Goode under age of twelve. Asks that writ of partition issue. Eliza Goode admx of Mackeness Goode decd & gdn of Susannah Goode will comply with decree of court. Land called Pools Muster ground on main road from Cambridge to Charleston on Halfway Swamp cannot be divided without injury to each. Received of Reeves Martin [money] in part of bond given by Martin for land formerly belong to John Pool 25 October 1819, Eliza Goode. Whit Brooks receipt to Reeves Martin for part payment of his bond. Recd two receipts of Mrs Eliza Goode 28 Oct 1819. W Brooks. The bond is now settled in full, the other money belonging to R Martin.

Edward Washington Wade vs Wm Garrett. Bill for discovery & relief. E W Wade's father Edward Wade of Halifax County, Virginia, possessed Negroes and lands. Made his will 12 February 1776, loaned wife Letty Wade all his estate until his daughter Betsy Wade attained age sixteen at which time his estate should be sold by his executors and the money equally divided between wife Letty Wade, daughter Betsy Marshall Wade, and his sons William Wade, Abraham Martin Wade, and Washington Wade your orator. In case any should die without lawful children that part of his estate should be equally divided among remaining children. William Stokes, William Rawlins, and Samuel Perrin his executors have died. About time Betsy Marshall Wade became sixteen, some Negroes were sold and other personal property for the payment of debts; the Negroes were bought in by the executors for the benefit of the children of sd Edward Wade and debts were paid. The Negroes so bought and other Negroes not sold were divided by sd executors instead of money. Negroes received by Abram Marshall Wade on the division were wench Tabby, man Harry, girl Mourning, children of Tabby, Anniky; about 1794 Abraham Martin Wade removed to Edgefield from Virginia; about 1806 he moved to Mississippi Territory until 27 July 1816 when he died without leaving a lawful heir. His Negroes have since increased and are in possession of divers persons, five in possession of William Garrett of this district. Betsy Marshal Wade has also died before Abraham Marshal Wade whereby your orator and sd William Wade are the only surviving children of Edward Wade. William Wade has relinquished claim to same to your Orator whereby he became solely entitled to same. He applied to William Garrett to deliver up sd Negroes and account for their hire since the death of sd Abraham Martin Wade but he has refused to do so. Ellison & Glascock. [no date]

Reply of William Garrett: he bought Negroes, was ignorant of manner in which Abraham Wade acquired and sold them without giving notice to purchasers, believes Edward W Wade knew of sale, prays dismissal. Sworn by Wm Garrett, 16 Jany 1818; Whit Brooks.

Verbatim Will of Edward Wade, Halifax County, [details as quoted above]. I appoint Memucan Hunt, William Stokes, William Rawlins and Samuel Perrin to be executors. 12 February 1776. /s/ Edward Wade. Wit Charles Wade, Wm Wade, P Moss, Anne Wade. "It appearing to the Court that the Camplainant has complete and adequate remedy at Law, it is ordered & decreed that his bill be dismissed with Costs."

Joseph Hackney, Polly his wife & John Cook vs Admrs of West Cook. Discovery & Account. John Talberd admr de bonis non of West Cook decd ads Joseph Hackney et al. Polly Hackney formerly Polly Cook, a dau of late West Cook decd, 18 December 1810 Bill of Complaint on behalf of themselves and of John Cook at that time a minor and one of the children of sd West Cook which sd John Cook your orator, Joseph Hackney guardian, against Charles Martin Esqr and Prudence his wife and George Y McMurphy admrs of goods and chattels of West

GENEALOGICAL ABSTRACT OF EDGEFIELD EQUITY COURT RECORDS

Cook for recount and distribution of personal estate of West Cook. West Cook died intestate
13 April 1808. [106 items] West Cook left Prudence Cook now Prudence Martin his widow
by whom he had no children, Polly Hackney, John Cook, Sally Cook who married John
Downey, Amanda Cook and Caroline Cook his only children by a former wife [Another page
lists heirs as Prudence the widow, Joseph Hackney and Polly his wife. John Cook, Amanda
Cook, Martha Cook, and Carolina Cook, John and Sally Downey, only children and coheirs].
George Y McMurphy demurred to sd Bill; answer filed 14 May 1811. Before further proceedings George Y McMurphy died about last day of March last past. Sd McMurphy had
made will in writing, his wife Kesiah McMurphy admx, William Mait[?] Esqr exr refused to
qualify; the sd extx proved sd will and took upon herself the admn of sd trust.... George Y
McMurphy admr as afsd of West Cook possessed himself of all whereby sd suit ought to be
served as against sd Kesiah extx afsd & sd John Talbot [also Talbert] appointed admr .
    Joseph Hackney et al vs Kesiah P McMurphy et al. Deft says her husband George
Y McMurphy and Mrs Prudence Cook widow of West Cook admr estate until McMurphy
was called out in service of his country in an expedition to the lower part of this state where
he died on or about the thirty first day of March 1814. Prudence Cook, admx, married
Charles Martin Esqr in December 1808, by virtue of his marital rights became entitled to one
third of property of sd West Cook. Estate greatly in debt; debts to estate not yet collected.
Negro women Charlotte and Pat had been sent to Hackney house to nurse West Cook's infant
children, two in care of Mrs. Hackney and one with Mrs Downey. John Downey had the
women appraised. Bacon, Dft's sol. /s/ Keziah P McMurphy, 23 May 1816; Whit Brooks.
    Report of Richd Rapley commissioner for Ninety Six Dist. 7 June 1811, finances.
    Joseph Hackney & wife vs John Talbert & others, 9 Jany 1817. Expences of Martha
Cook, Caroline Cook, John Cook, M Simpson. Testimony of Joseph Fuller about Negro girls
Pat and Charlotte age about 18 to 20, fellow Ned. Prudence Cook married Charles Martin
and became administrator until he left for Mississippi Territory in Dec 1810.
    Account of sale certified a true copy by John Simkins, Ordinary, 8 February 1811.
John Searle[Negro man Robbin], Catht Cauley [Negro man Toney bought first by Henry
Martin and resold on account of his not complying with terms of sale], William King, Saml
Shannon, Isaac Haws, Edmd Killercade, H A Nixon, Elisha Whitten, John Lamar, Reuben
Pierce, Ambrose Price, John Hardy, Philip Holt, William Price. Geo Y Macmurphy admr.
    Sales 11-13 Jany 1809 to Charles Martin [Negroes Gabe, Ned, Edy, old Tom, Cyrus,
Pompey. George. Mariah], William Cox, Edmond Halliman, Pleasant Benning, Edward
Holmes, Thos Scarborough, James Owensby, Christopher Cox, William Garrett [man Jack],
Thos Martin [Negro Prince], William Jeter, [Negro Davy] Benjamin Glover [Negro Andrew],
Charles McKie [Negro Sam], John Downey [Negro George, Isaack, woman Nancy], Joseph
Hackney [woman Minte and three children subject to claim of Robt Z Cook], William
Newsom [woman Phebe, boy Bob], George Y McMurphy, Martin & McMurphy, George W
Evans, John Talbert, William Robertson, Anselm Talbert, James Martin, John Holsonback,
Robert Jennings, Martin Rose, Thomas Jackson, Jacob Holsonback, Wyley Price, Cavington
Searles, Mackerness Minter, Harmon Copher, James Pickett, Thomas Martin, John Moore
[Negro Tom and his wife Delcey, boy Dick, Friday, man Tom], Abiah Morgan, Thos H Howl,
Daniel New, Henry Martin, Geo Ganes[?], Frederick Lewis[?Lairs?]. Receipts: 16 July 1814
rec'd of K P McMurphy my distributive share of estate of West Cook decd /s/ Thos P
Simpson. Rec'd of Mrs McMurphy 10 Jan 1815, John Cook. Recd of Mrs Kesiah P

McMurphy extx estate of G Y McMurphy decd an account proven against Miss Amanda Cook; John Talbert Admr estate of W Cook decd. Promissory notes of Ths Adams 30 January 1808 wit by N H Bugg. [other financial records]. Statement of John Talbert that Joseph Hackney resides witihout the limits of this state, 3 June 1817; A Edmunds JP. George Y McMurphy admr West Cook vs David Mims, Thomas Cobb et al. Dismissed.

FILM NO. JR.4068, Files 11-20

#11 Sarah Quarles Hammond vs Frances Julia Hammond, Andrew Jackson Hammond by guardian Charles Hammond, William Hammond not found, Eliza Hammond, Leroy Hammond, Ann Hammond, and John Hammond junior. Filed 10 January 1817. Sarah Quarles Hammond widow of Col. Leroy Hammond, claim of dower in land Leroy Hammond in his lifetime purchased of Leroy Hammond jr; Writ of admeasurement issued,Charles Hammond. Commissioners Lewis L Hammond, Jeremiah Bussey & Alexander Stewart are of opinion that land cannot be divided to do equal justice to all parties, 26 May 1818. 20 May 1812 Recd of LeRoy Hammond Senr $180 in full for 1000 acres on Horse Creek originally granted to LeRoy Hammond adj Ezekiel Roebucks land; /s/ LeRoy Hammond Jr; wit. Jas Levingston. Certification from William J Bunce, editor, Augusta Herald, that he published in his paper From September 13 to December 30 a notice to William Hammond to answer above bill. Bill for dower, sundry tracts, 42 acres on Savannah River at New Richmond, 200 acres part of 240 acres originally granted to James Martin, two parts of tract originally granted to Benjamin Allen, 50 acres part of land originally granted to Elizabeth Miller, 1000 acres on Kines fork of Horse creek bought of Leroy Hammond Jr by Col Leroy Hammond but for which no titles were executed; writ of admeasurement to issue for all above lands.

#12 James Hix vs Joseph Jennings admr of Dickenson Jennings decd and guardian of Caroline Jennings under age of fourteen. Bill for partition, June 1818. James Hix married widow Jane Jennings, two children John and Caroline one of which is since dead. Under marital rights he is entitled to share of Dickenson Jennings land on Fish creek of Savannah River adj Joseph Jennings, James Pickets land. Land to be sold, 5 June 1818; Whit Brooks.

#13 Walter Taylor vs John Clark, Mary Burney, Abraham Ardis, [blank] Mills and John Sturzenegger. Bill for discovery to account [4 pages badly torn, ink bled through, can't read].

[Appears to be #14 David Mims exr vs Thomas P Martin guardian. Answer of David Mims executor estate of Samuel Scott senior decd to complaint of Thomas P Martin as guardian of John Allen Scott Martin. minor under age 21. Samuel Scott senior died possessed of considerable real and personal estate. A copy of his will is filed by plf; among executors therein named this dft alone qualified; dft carried will into effect by having sales of personal estate 28 February and 1 March 1809 and of real estate on 19th June 1809 on credit of twelve months, the two amounts of sales making only $7457.89 1/2. Armstead Burt, who married the widow of Samuel C Scott, a son of the testate, commenced suit before this dft had collected or could have collected the principal part of debts due the estate, final determination February term 1813 where accounts and vouchers produced by dft were so satisfactory that were not even questioned by court or counsel Further states that John A S Martin, ward of Thomas P. was entitled to precisely the same sum that sd Armstead Burt in his capacity as guardian was entitled. Negroes Peter, Nell, and Jenny had been bequeathed to sd John A S Martin by his grandfather sd Samuel Scott. Asks suit be dismissed. Sworn by David Mims; 8 April 1817 Whit Brooks. Simkins & McDuffie dfts sols.

[Seems continuation of #13] John Clarke & others ads Walter Taylor. Answer of Dr. Thomas Mills, deft to Bill of complaint of Walter Taylor. Dft hath lately married Mary Ann Bender eldest daughter of George Bender who was married to one of the daughters of Ann Zubly as stated in the Bill; Mills is ignorant of charges as to management of her property. George Bender is dead, his will appointed Abraham Ardis, Craddock Burnell, Gasper Naile and Daniel Naile executors thereof. Equally ignorant of what the estate of George Bender may be entitled to of sd Ann Zublys estate. Sworn Barnwell District, 28 September 1815 by T Mills; Chas Goodwin JP.

Answer of Abram Ardis to Bill of Complaint of Walter Taylor. Abram Ardis married Sarah, a daughter of Ann Zubly after Sarah was widow of George Bender, Ann Zubly died leaving married daughters and possessed of property to what amount this deft is ignorant, also ignorant of doings of complainant or of John Clarke as admr in her estate, knows not whether he is entitled to anything in right of his wife from sd estate, leaves it to Court to protect his wife's interest therein, admits he was named one of tlhe executors in the will of George Bender jointly with Craddock Burnell, Gasper Nail and Daniel Nail who all qualified. Sworn Barnwell District, /s/ Abram Ardis, 28 September 1815. Chas Goodwin JP.

Answer of Mary Burney one of the dfts to Bill of Complaint of Walter Taylor. She is a daughter of Ann Zubly; she married William Burney who is since dead, she is ignorant of the charges and allegations relative to her mothers estate or the doings of the admrs thereto except that before her marriage she received money, cannot recall the amount, from Jonathan Myers in part for one years rent of part of the tract of land belonging to her mother's estate which she believes rented at nineteen pounds a year; she believes her husband received the balance of rent ; she hath not administered in her husbands estate but submits her rights to the court. Sworn Barnwell District 28 September 1815; /s/ Mary Burney. Chas Goodwin UQ.

Walter Taylor vs Jno Clark & others. From 1796 to this date estate of small amount and easy administration, yet they have been rendered by admrs whose foresight does not appear to have contemplated the time when they would be called upon to account. So great is the confusion which has been occasioned by the joint admn of Jno Clark and Walter Taylor & so imperfect the returns to the Ordinary that to ascertain the precise amount due to each distributee is at this time impossible. The estate of Ann Zubley which is the estate in dispute sold in 1796 for $967.12 ½ which was distributable among the five children of Mrs Zubley: Eleanor Zubley married John Clarke, Ann married Walter Taylor, Sarah now Mrs Ardis, Mary now Mrs Burney, Charlotte now Mrs. Sturzenegger. Great part of estate appropriated to debts and legatees. In what manner plantation rents & profits have been disposed of by admrs does not appear from papers submitted to inspection. 29 Jany 1818. Jno Simkins

Answer of John Clarke. Complainant hath in his sole possession the account book; he hath refused either to give it or to shew it to him though demanded; dft states that complainant hath also a small trunk containing the estate papers or some of them and which he should be compelled to produce. Ann Zubly died possessed of one tract of land; the rents of which he believes have been distributed but in what proportion and whether to the full amount he cannot recollect nor can he until there is a full settlement of affairs of the estate.

GENEALOGICAL ABSTRACT OF EDGEFIELD EQUITY COURT RECORDS

With respect to William Burney having received his full proportion of the estate he states that he paid him to the amount of $84.95 himself and took his receipt for same which hath since been lost. Barnwell District, 23 September 1818; /s/ John Clarke. Chas Goodwin UQ.

John Clarke & others ads Walter Taylor. Answer of John Sturzenegger to bill of Walter Taylor. Says he and complainant administered Ann Zubly's estate; five daughters; denies he has any part of his distributive share of sd estate unless his wife received it before his marriage with her. Edgefield Dist, 7 August 1815; /s/ John Sturzenegger; Whit Brooks.

[no number] Copy of will of Benjamin Darby certified 2 Jany 1819 by M Simkins OED, 6 December 1814; David Cogburn to take charge of my three children William, Martha, James; estate except Negro girl Rachel to David Cogburn until children come of age, then to be equally divided; Cogburn to sell such of my estate, except Negroes, as to advantage of my children. Estate, except Negroes, for raising and educating my three children; Rachel to be given to my mother; David Cogburn executor. Wit. Abner Landrum.

Walter Taylor vs Jno Clarke. Bill for Settlement. Ordered matters of amount involved be referred to Commissioner of Edgefield District; that he report to next session this court; W Thompson, 4 May 1816. Financial matters[selections]: Paid Francis Volaton for shoes for Charlotte; Pd estate of John E Smith for printing; Pd John Simkins for examining accounts from 1796 to 1800, Walter Taylor admr. Pd D K Baerd for Charlotte; Pd J Pryor exr of John Pryor decd. Paid Joseph Butlers acct. Cummings store. Dr. Williamson. Paid Oliphant for Shinholser. Pd Howel & Hix for beef. Pd S. Mays for tax. Pd Collin Rodgers. Pd Mrs. Galphin for board. Pd Negro Jim for bottoming chairs. Pd Martin for mending Polleys saddle. Pd John Savage. 15 May 1799 by note in favour estate of Ann Zubly against estate of Casper Nail Senr. 1802 Feb 20, pd Boru[Boxie?] dancingmaster for Charlotte. Pd John Sturzenegger. Pd Elizabeth Sturzenegger. Jonathan Myer, candlestick. Wm Tobler, cattle. Giles Bowers, mare. Archibald Hatcher, flock of geese. Casper Nail, old Negro wench. John Winham, loom. Abraham Ardis, waggon & geers. Alexr Downer, rake. Walter Taylor, hogshead. James Richards, grinding stone. John Clarke, corn. Geo Bender, cow. Laml Young, pot. Saml Burgess, cattle. Jno Oliphant. Mr Tutt, recording titles. Pd J Moore, tax. Pd Jno Meyers, brandy. Pd William Niely for schooling Charlotte.

No. 14. Stephen Garrett vs Jeremiah Wilborn admr of Peter Farrer Jr. Bill for injunction and relief. About two years ago Peter Farrar Senr pledged to Garrett Negro boy London then quite small as security for payment of $247 which Garrett paid in discharge of prior mortgage on sd Negro; took out mortgage on other Negroes since dead, Garrett has never received payment. Jeremiah Willborn admr of Peter Farrar Jr brought action on alleged verbal gift of sd Negro to Peter Farrar Jr by his grandfather the sd Peter Farrar Sr about 20 years ago, whch sd gift was not accompanied by delivery but Negro remained in possession of Peter Farrar sr wherby he was enabled to commit fraud upon subsequent purchasers & mortgagers. If he had really made the gift afsd did defraud your orator but your orator thinks it extremely doubtful whether a gift was ever made to Peter Farrar Jr. The only evidence of it were declarations of Peter Farrar from which the presiding judge at the trial of the above action charged jury was doubtful evidence on which to support the gift. Garrett states that jury found verdict for plaintiff and that execution has issued against Garrett. He states that three years ago when about to leave the state, took from Peter Farrar Sr a written mortgage of this Negro previous to claim set up by admr of Peter Farrar Jr. Peter Farrar Jr died about 16 years ago. Garrett has been in possession of sd Negro for 10 years, and old Peter Farrar 6, yet this claim has lain dormant until 2 years ago when Willborn admrd estate of Peter Jr. Your orator was prevented by rules of common law from availing himself of fair presumption arising from length of time during which interested parties suffered their claim to be dormant. His mortgage has never been foreclosed on afsd Negro who was not worth more than $247 first advanced, and is not now worth more than the two sums advanced by your orator to sd Peter Sr and legal interest thereon. Believes alleged gift is set up to defraud auditors of Peter Farrar Sr [page torn]. Simkins & McDuffie Complainants sols. Sworn 18 April 1817; /s/ Stephen Garrett.

Answer of Samuel Wilbourn. Does not believe that Peter Farrow Sr mortgaged sd Negro or that he was indebted to Stephen Garrett, believes Stephen indebted to him; accounts against Stephen in favor of Peter Farrow to amount of $438.50. Dft admits that suit was commenced by this dft as admr of the estate of Peter Farrow Jr and judgment ordered in favor of dft. Dft believes the Negro was delivered and was in possesison of Peter Farrow previous many years at the house of Mrs Rivers his grandmother.... Ellison dfts dol. Sworn 3 Feby 1818; /s/ Jeremiah Wellborn.

Bond of Stephen Garrett and Jeremiah Hatcher to Jeremiah Wilborn admr of Peter Farrar Jr, 12 May 1817; witness Mark McHan[McLane?]. Peter Farrar Jr obtained verdict for $900 against Stephen Garrett. Garrett having filed bill with Court of Equity and obtained injunction from Judge Desassure, Stephen Garrett shall abide by final decree of this court & shall obey whatever court orders without delay, above obligation to be void.

Stephen Garrett to Peter Farrar Dr: to work of Negro wench six year $325; to work of Linder seven year, $280. Jeff Sharpton proved 4 days attendance 8 Mar 1817; A Edmonds.

File Number 15, missing. Will be filmed later if found.

File #16 Cross bill. 4 June 1816. John Sturzenegger admr with will annexed of John Joachim Tobler decd, Alexander Hannah and wife Ann which Ann was widow of sd John J Tobler and admx with John Sturzenegger, and Adeline Tobler, minor, daughter of John Joachim Tobler by her next friend John Sturzenegger against Bryant Marsh admr estate of Elisha Bryant. Bryant filed bill against John Sturzenegger and Ann Hannah before her marriage with the sd Alexander as admr & admx and also against Casper Nail exr of will of William Tobler decd. John Joachim Tobler and William Tobler were admrs of estate of Elisha. Charges admrs with having money belonging to sd estates.[lengthy quotation from William Tobler's will. Provided for maintenance and emancipation of two old Negroes Windsor and Kate. Sole management of estate to John Joachim Tobler my brother; at his death to Gasper Nail, then to be equally divided amongst his child or children and William and Elisha Bryant my nephews share and share alike but shares not to be delivered until they shall respectively attain age 21years.] Charge that Bryant Marsh and Casper Nail confederating against heirs.

Answer of Casper Neal. William Tobler died without lawful issue; John J Tobler died; this respondant managed estate of William Tobler decd, does not know if Wm and John J Tobler acted conjointly in admn estate of Elisha Bryant, or confusion in management of the estate of Elisha Bryant accounts. 8 November 1816 /s/ Casper Nail. Chas Goodwin JQ

Bryan Marsh admr of Elisha Bryan and guardian of his minor child. By William Tobler's will, William Tobler Bryan, only surviving child of sd Elisha Bryan whose guardian this dft is, became entitled to vested interest in Wm Tobler's estate when he becomes 21. Simkins & McDuffie dfts sol. /s/ B Marsh. 11 May 1816; Whit Brooks.

Ordered that cause be referred to Commissioner to enquire into debts due by estate of Wm Tobler, and what part thereof were paid by J J Tobler, and what part of William Tobler's estate J J Tobler received in his life, account for rents & profits of that estate.

#17   John Allen Scott Martin son of Charles Martin by his guardian Thomas R Martin. vs David Mims. Samuel Scott, grandfather of orator, by will 21 January 1809 devised to orator three Negroes. Estate in SC and Georgia to be sold by exrs and divided into five equal parts, one fifth of which devised to your orator John Allen Scott Martin. Shares of the under age to be put out on interest for benefit of infants. John Middleton and George Graves refused to act. David Mims became executor. Sold real estate, $20,000. Did not put the money out at interest, defeating benefit intended. Filed 24 December 1810[1816?]. Will of Samuel Scott. Dau Sarah Mims, Negroes Old Dick and Northward Dick. Dau Mary Graves Negroes Andrew and Cloey. Dau Elizabeth Middleton, Negroes Sam & Curry. Grandchildren Elizabeth Scott, John Scott, Samuel Scott children of Samuel C Scott decd Negroes Hall, Amy, Judy. Grandson John Allen Scott Martin Negroes Peter, Nel, Jenny. Of estate, John Allen Scott Martin one share. Elizabeth, John & Samuel Scott one share. 21 January 1809. Wit John Boyd, James Buist, Mary Scott. True copy, 15 July 1812. /s/ Jno Simkins OED.

Receipt for $1675.25, August 20, 1814. /s/ Thomas P Martin, guardian for John A S Martin. Wit Abram Giles Dozier, J McCrackan. Settlement with Thomas P Martin, guardian of John A S Martin, Nov 22, 1815. /s/ John S Jeter atty for Thomas P Martin guardian of John A S Martin, November 23, 1815. Witness Abram Giles Dozier.

Dear Ellison. Having it not in my power to attend at Edgefield I wish you to attend to my little business there in the case against Tolbert, am indifferent whether it is off the docket or not as I have never received one cent for attending to it and [illegible surname] has left the state. The case of Martin against Mims I wish you to have the acct of reference extended, and to argue the only point in the case whether Mims is not bound to pay interest while the money remained in his hands, as executor. Mr Brooks will shew you the bill and exhibit there with files from which you can obtain every information necessary. There was a cross bill filed in the case of Marsh against Sturzenegger and others. The cross bill was filed against Marsh and Casper Neal by Sturzenegger, I wish you also to attend to Neals interest in the case as I was employed and filed his answer to the Bill. However Mr Bacon was also employed by Mr Neal, by attending to the above you will much oblige your friend Wm Lomax.

No. 18 John Parks Bacon & wife Mary and your orator Thomas alias TomMcKie vs Edward Wade and others. James Lamar died leaving his sisters Mary Bacon wife of John P Bacon and Mrs Sarah Wade wife of Edward Washington Wade, and Charles Lamar his brother who were entitled each to a third of the property. By advice of Richard Johnston at whose house James Lamar died, and to avoid expense of Ltrs of Admn, came to amicable and fair division of property. Tom McKie purchased land, erected a mill and other buildings, in debt to distributees to amount of purchase money. Before title was made someone refused to make title and possessed themselves of Negroes and property which fell to John P and Mary Bacon. Edward W Wade and wife Sarah allege that Richard Johnson, after division and sale, brought forward a nuncupative will of James Lamar by which he left his property to Richard Johnston in trust for children of Sarah Wade: Sarah B, Edward, Drayton, Martin, Johnson R, & Mary Wade. James Lamar's widow now Mrs Polly Johnson wife of Richard Johnson was a witness. The Ordinary granted probate. John P Bacon and wife Mary reside without the limit of this State, were not notified. Bacon, complts solr.

Answer of Mary Johnson extx of Richard Johnson decd who was trustee and extr of James Lamar who died 1714. Richard Johnson advised equal division of estate of James Lamar and of Edward Lamar who died shortly after. She is confident that her deceased husband never saw Bacon or Wade or their wives from death of James Lamar until division of estate. James Lamar made nuncupative will, spoken 3 or 4 days before his death, to which she was a witness and which was reduced to writing by James Miller the same day. Her deceased husband made no secret of the nuncupative will which was known others besides witnesses. Altho living 17 miles from E W Wade and 40 from J P Bacon she does not believe that her decd husband announced the existence of such a will to either of them. Simkins & McDuffie. Sworn 15 July 1816; /s/ Mary (x) Johnson.

Answer of Charles Lamar. Division of the estate was much to dissatisfaction of E W Wade and wife who felt entitled to certain Negroes of Edward Lamar (for his estate was to be divided with James Lamars) which were allotted to J P Bacon so much that this defeated the division from being final. Previous to the division deft heard report of nuncupative will made by James Lamar but he placed no confidence in it and was told by Capt Richard Johnson subsequently that altho he made no secret of sd nuncupative will, yet he had been kept from making a positive declaration of it because he thought justice would be done by division among themselves which would rid him in his advanced years of a trouble and responsibility. Dft states he is far from nullifying sd nuncupative will; believes it was a fair expression of his brother's desires. Simkins & McDuffie Dfts sol. Sworn 20 Decr 1816; /s/ Ths Lamar.

Answer of Edward W Wade and wife Sarah. There never was final adjustment. Had only a report of a nuncupative will made by James Lamar. Could hardly give credit to as Capt Richard Johnson had never informed them of such will; they agreed to deeamong themselves the property of James Lamar and of Edward Lamar who died shortly after him. Difficulties arose to ascertain directly from Captain Johnson whether there was reality in this reported nuncupative will which they had been kept from enquiring into; they thought Capt Johnson would have informed them, they wrote to sd Capt R Johnston to ascertain the fact who replied that such a will existed but he thought it might have been settled in the way they attempted. As to sale of land to Thos McKie, one of the pl, they are perfectly content with the sale having received their third of the purchase money and made titles to sd Tom McKie. Dfts had the three Negroes left by James Lamar: Charles age 18 or 19, Bob about same age, Little Cargie size 1, and Lewis about 14. /s/ E W Wade, /s/ Sarah Wade, 15 July 1816.

Mrs Mary Johnson ads John P Bacon & others. Inventory, estate of James Lamar, 29 May 1815. /s/ Saml Marsh, Fed Swearengen, Benja Haleker, John Swearengen.

John P Bacon & wife & Thomas MCKie vs Edwd W Wade & wife & others, June 1867. Opens probate of nuncupative will of James Lamar hitherto proved before the Ordinary; to have benefit of agreement made between heirs of James Lamar; confirmation of contract by heirs of James Lamar to Thomas McKie. No doubt of nuncupative will's having been

17

made by James Lamar before four witnesses. No evidence of definitive division of the estate; the arrangements were broken off. Verbal agreement was made before parties were apprized of their rights. No difficulty as to sale of land. Real estate of James Lamar could not pass by nuncupative will. It was divisible among his two sisters and his brother as his heirs. They have agreed to sell & have actually sold it to Mr McKie who has possession and has paid part of the purchase money and received titles from some heirs, those parties who have not yet made titles do so. Henry W DeSaussure. No date.

Sale of property of Edward and James Lamar, 4 June 1815. Buyers Tom McKie, Edward Hampton, Shurly Whatly Jr, Jno C Garrett, Benj Tutt, Dempsey Bussey, Miss Polly Wil---, Thomas Cobb, Charles Lamar, Alexr Edmunds, William Drukam[?], Mrs Griffis, Edward W Wade, Butler Williams, Thomas H Howle, Wyatt Taylor, Nicholas Fox, Thomas Marbry,John Cleveland, Chesley Farrar, George G A Gage, Robert Levingston, Miss Elizabeth Wright. /s/ Abraham Joust.

No. 19. Harman W Bozeman and wife Nancy late Nancy Burnett and William Burnett by his next friend sd Harman W Bozeman. On 6 September 1810 Harman married Nancy Bozeman late Nancy Burnett dau of Thomas Burnett who died intestate in 1797 possessed of estate and crop then unsold leaving children, each entitled to one seventh of two thirds of his estate. On 1 January 1798 widow Mary Burnett mother of Nancy and William, took out ltrs/admn on estate of her decd husband with Wm Quarles and David Quarles securities. She made no returns; October 1800 after death of Mary Burnett, who had married Ephraim Ferrel, William Quarles and James Quarles (the latter has since died) took out ltrs/admn on estate of Thomas Burnett; took possession of undivided property of Mary Ferrel in estate of her decd husband and intestate Thomas Burnett; which oratrix, oarator, and other five children are entitled to. Mary Ferrell having also died intestate on 24 November 1800, sd William Quarles admr sold personal property for $4560.42. Orator and Oratrix charge that their decd father's estate being well adapted to culture of Tobacco and cotton ought to have produced considerable sum by annual rent of same from 1800 when Wm Quarles took possession to present. Ask equitable distribution of personal property in hands of William Quarles together with rents.

Report of Commr Whit Brooks. Accounts 24 Novr 1800 to June 1817. Wm Quarles rec'd since settlement with Jas Quarles the guardian of Nancy Burnett now Nancy Bozeman money which could not have been embraced in that settlement. Ask Writ of Partition to lay off to William Burnett his part of real estate, no date. Appraisers John Roper, Benj Roper.

Five- page statement of William Quarles sworn July 1816; /s/ William Quarles with amendment 4 February 1817; /s/ William Quarles. [Cannot be read on microfilm because of discoloration and bleeding of ink].

Bond of James and William Quarles, Joseph Fuller, and Richard Quarles, 29 October 1800; James and William Quarles to administer estate of Thomas Burnett; Jno Simkins OED; Stephen Norris.

Decree, June 1817. Question of an agreement made between Ephraim Ferrel and four older children of Thomas Burnett by which agreement not satisfied. /s/ Henry W DeSaussure.

Estate of Thomas Burnett and Mary Ferrel decd account with James and William Quarles admrs., Feb 1803. Paid William Hale, William Brazer, Joseph Hightower, Simkins, Thom Burnett, for boarding and clothing Nancy Burnett. June 1802; Paid Wm Tennant, Stephen Norris, David Quarles, Charles Old Esq, Thomas Burnett Junr, Jonathan Moore,

William Hall, Thomas Garrett, Ephraim Ferrel, Nicholas Cooper, Edmond Woods, Richard Tutt Esqr, Leroy Hammond, William Watson, Polly Burnett, Nancy Burnett, William Burnett, John Longmire, Charles Hammond, David Roper, Charles Roper, John Wills, James Baker, Benja Harvy, John Simkins, Richard Witherington for William Garrett August 1802.

Accounts 20 Novr 1806, paid John Wills, Allen Anderson, Eugene Brenan.

Property sold 24 November 1800: pd William Hall, Nicholas Woods, Benjamin Mack, Freeman Hardy, David Moore, Samuel Quarles, David Roper Senr, Seth Howard, West Cook, Ephraim Ferrel, Charles Lamar, Eason Drake, Enos Howard, Isaac Randolph, John Green, Zachary Smith, William Ellis, Barzel Garner, Robert Cammack, John Wright, Cader Curry, Willis Whatley, James Jones,

Agreement, Ephraim Ferrel, 28 October 1800. William Hall, John Wells, Thomas Burnett agree to pay to four younger children of Mary Ferrell decd Two hundred Dollars quit claim to my portion of the estate of Mary Ferrell. /s/ Ephraim Ferrell, 28 October 1800. Witness: Samuel Quarles, Richard Quarles. Undersigned heirs of Mary Ferrel decd promise to pay the four younger children of Mary Ferrel Two hundred Dollars, 28 October 1800; William Hall, John Wills, Thos Burnett, James Quarles for Thos Burnett. Wit Richard Quarles, Samuel Quarles. Proven 29 October 1800 by Richard Quarles. Rec 4 Jany 1801.

Accounts November 1804: Paid William Lewis, John Wills, James Quarles for Nancy Burnetts legacy & interest on same; William Quarles admr

No. 20 Mrs Ann Taylor by her next friends John Clarke and Abraham Ardis agt Walter Taylor Esq, Bill for separate maintenance. Sworn 13 September 1810; /s/ Anne Taylor; John Newman J P, Barnwell District. Petition gives insight into social conditions in the Beach Island area of Edgefield District. Unprotected lives of married women are sharply delineated against, by inference, the power of husbands. Ann Zubly married Walter Taylor in 1786. She had three children of whom only Agnes Ann Taylor survived. About 1799 Anne's husband began to mistreat her, falsely accusing her of infidelities. The husband beat her with a loaded whip, dragged her by the hair, blackened her eyes, broke a rib, choked her, f logged her with a hickory, punched her face, loosened a tooth. A male witness observed that they had frequent quarrels "commonly begun by her." The judge wrote, "Regardless that she was at fault.... the flinging of his knife and fork across the table at her before company, and the knocking of her down with a stool before his own father, have all been proved satisfactorily and are instances of outrageous conduct seldom witnessed in civilized society." She said she feared to go home. "It is hardly to be conceived that she would have taken refuge in such a filthy asylum as the vault of a necessary or that she would have jumped over the sharp pointed pailings of a garden unless she had been urged by some terrible fears." The dft pay one third of his real income as alimony to the wife, to commence from the present day, to be payable on the 18th day of October, April, half yearly until in the opinion of this court the complt may return in safety to her husband. Therefore let it be referred to the commr to ascertain the one third of the dfts income and let the dft pay the cost of this suit. W. James, Columbia, 15 Decr 1810.

Witnesses and other persons mentioned are [husband=Walter Taylor; wife=Ann] John Clarke, wife's brother-in law; Allen Nesbitt, wife's son-in-law; William Burney, husband of wife's youngest sister Polly; Mrs Ramsay, widow of late Judge Ramsay; Martha Taylor, husband's cousin; Mrs Bracket, husband's sister; Mr James Panton, Mrs Bender, now Mrs Abraham Ardis, wife's sister; David Taylor of Savannah, husband's cousin; slave Nance;

James Taylor, husband's uncle; Dr. Walter Taylor and wife Ann of Savannah, husband's uncle; Mrs Schaffer; Hugh Nesitt, little son of Allen and Agnes Nesbitt; Mrs Daniel Neal; Mrs Flint husband's sister; John Brackett husband's nephew; Mrs. Burney, wife's sister; Justice John Newman of Branwell district; John Caldwell, Sheriff of Abbeville District; W Garrett; Hugh Nisbet; Dr. Anderson Watkins, Mrs Sturzenegger, wife's sister; Mrs Meyers, wife's cousin; --- Barnett; overseer --- Bates; Mrs Williams; overseer John Fleming; Mr Shinholster; Mr Neal; Mr Carstaffin[?]; Jerry Minor; Mr. Thoms Galphin; Rev James Halcombe; --- Bevans; Mr Goodman.

The answer of Walter Taylor, defendant, sworn 16 March 1811; /s/ Walter Taylor. Jas Wardlaw Clk & JQ. Walter Taylor ads Ann Taylor, 22 March 1811; Yancey, Dfts Solr. Answer of Mrs Susannah Taylor of Burke County, Georgia. She has known Walter Taylor for 40 years and Mrs Ann Taylor for 20 years; Heard Charlotte Zubly now Mrs Jno Sturzenegger reprove Ann for imprper language; /s/ Susanna Taylor; Abraham Twiggs JC.

Henry C Ashton vs Lewis Cantelou, Amy Thorn vs Ch & C Thorn. Solr Lucas vs Wm Nichols. Subpoena John Clarke Esqr, Mrs Ann Taylor, Elihu Williams to Abbeville Courthouse 19 April 1811. Giles Bowers proves four days attendance and 148 miles in behalf of Mrs Ann Taylor, 14 June 1811 before Jas Wardlaw, Clk. John Clarke proves 4 days attendance and 70 miles travel, 14 June 1811. Interrogations put to Mary Shaffer, Georgia. Subpoena to Mrs Helena Clarke, Mrs Sarah Ardis, Mrs Charlotte Sturzenegger, Miss Polly Bender; Richard Andrew Rapley commr in Equity, 19 April 1811. Mrs Polly Bender proves 4 days attendance and 70 miles travel; 15 June 1811; /s/ Mary Ann Bender. Answers of Hugh Nesbitt: July or August last was with Dft in his house; he said she[Ann] left the house, he did not abuse her other than by a kick or shove of foot which did not put her off her feet. She is a virtuous woman; /s/ Hugh Nesbitt, Augusta, Georgia, 6 June 1811. James Panton 14 June 1811 proves 4 days attendandance and 70 miles. Mrs Margaret Flint, 7 June 1811, Augusta, Richmond County, Georgia, thought Ann Taylor used insulting language to her husband. /s/ Margaret Flint. Interrogation of John Taylor. Walter Taylor is my son and he is now 48 to 50 years of age; saw dft throw a stool which struck her on the breast which occasioned her to fall back on the floor; Augusta, Georgia, June 6, 1811; John Neilson, John Camplace, Tom White.

#21   David Cogburn vs William Ellison and others filed 31 May 1816. Judges of State Equity Court Hon Henry William Desaussure, Theodore Gaillard, Thomas Waters, William James, Waddy Thompson. David Cogburn states that Benjamin Darby decd was possessed of 130 acres situate on Beaver Dam Creek near Edgefield Court House which he purchased from Thomas Winn and which Winn purchased from John Bolton. Benj Darby sold sd land to Wm Ellison for Two dollars fifty cents pr acre, part paid, remainder to be paid when titles made to land per bond executed by Benj Darby December 1814 binding Darby to make titles to land by 1 January 1815. Benjamin Darby died 26 December 1814 leaving three minor children, your orator by his will made guardian of his children. Benjn Darby also purchased of Rebecca Beams 56 acres on road from Edgefield Court House to Charleston about three miles from the Courthouse . Darby's will bequeathed all his property to be equally divided among his children: William Darby, Martha Darby & James Darby except one Negro woman Rachel whom he left to his mother, and a horse by a nuncupative will given to your orator. David Cogburn authorized by will to sell his property except his Negro as he should think most to advantage of his children to be given to his mother for raising and educating of his children; will not executed according to law. Sd land should be sold, land small and of inferior quality and would increase but little in value by remaining unsold until children should come of age. Orator is desirous of removing with sd children to the frontier settlements of the western country where he expects to better their condition as well as his own, but is unable to do so untill a sale of lands can be effected. Asks that William Ellison, William Darby, Martha Darby & James Darby appear before court. Glascock, complts sol.

William Ellison ads David Cogburn, 21 May 1816, answer. Ellison ready at any time to comply with contract. William Darby, Martha Darby and James Darby by guardian ad litem James Darby answer to David Cogburn. Minors incapable of making titles to land sold to William Ellison. William Ellison & James Darby sworn make oath that statements are true. /s/ W Ellison. /s/ James (x) Darby. Whit Brooks comr.

Wm Ellison ads D Cogburn. David Cogburn vs James Darby & others. Bill for relief. To advantage of minor children that land be sold. /s/ Whit Brooks comr. Deed Rebecca Beams to Benjn Darby 50 acres on road from Edgefield Courthouse to Piney Woods House originally granted to Nathan White adj Saml Walker, estate of Fredk Tillman decd, Stephen Tillman Jr. /s/ Rebecca Beams. Wit William Garganus, Joseph Eddins.

#22   William Jeter, Jno B Jeter et al vs Robert Glover. William Jeter, Jas J Jeter et al vs Robert Glover. 12 July 1816. Rebecca Glover and her children Elvira, Robert D and Charles Glover by their next friends sd William Jeter and John Jeter. Rebecca Jeter daughter of sd William and sister of sd John married Robert Glover and lived with him until his conduct towards her--cruel, intolerable beatings--compelled her to seek refuge in the decline of life under the roof of her father. Separation in January 1810[unsure of date as edge of page is torn]. January 1810 she returned, sd Glover executed deed to sd William and John Jeter as trustees of Rebecca Glover and her children conveying to them 100 acres good quality land and one third of all Negroes and future increase then owned by sd Robert Glover; reservation by which sd Robert Glover could continue the enjoyment so long as sd Rebecca should continue to reside with him. She submitted to barbrous treatment from her husband with resignation until being in imminent danger she fled to house of Mathew Mays wither she was pursued by Robert Glover; she is now residing with her father together with her children. This separation to be perpetual. Asks decree in favor of complainant, and that deed afsd be enforced. Jno J Jeter, sol.

Robert Glover to Wm Jeter & John Jeter. Deed of Trust. Filed 5 Feby 1810. Filed with commr 12 July 1816. Provisions as afsd. /s/ Robert Glover. Wit Zachariah Martin, Joel Martin. Proved by Zachariah Martin 23 January 1810; Richard Gantt QU. Rec 5 Feb 1810.

#23   William Thomas vs John Boyd guardian and others. Partition. Simkins & McDuffie plffs sols. Filing 28th May 1816. James Thomas died; widow Elizabeth, children: Silas (since died unmarried), John, Joice, Elizabeth, James & Sarah all of full age except Elizabeth and Sarah for whom Rev John Boyd has been guardian; also possessed of personal and real estate, his will in full force, inventory made 29 March 1805, $4486.62 ½, the widow takes all property during life except specific legacies. She died shortly after his death. Personal property was sold 29 February 1816, Negroes excepted. Negroes to be divided: Peter, Isaac, Jude, Nancy & child Bob, Harry, Spencer, Eliza, Ceiley, Aggy, Maria, Mary, George,

Terry, Curry, Will, James, Beiner, Eliza and Edy. John Thomas has sold his interest and received payment for same. The deceased James Thomas was possessed of land, 100 acres granted to S Jackson on Savannah River near Bull Sluice, Allen Robinson, LeRoy Hammond, purchased from James Johnson of Savannah; also a tract granted to Andrew Robinson 300 acres adj above tract on resurvey short of that quantity, together only 269 acres. Also 350 acres adj John Middleton, Thomas Meriwether, Daniel McKee, John Middleton purchased from Edward Prince, Thomas Clark, and Mrs [blank] Calliham; all subject to distribution. Joice Thomas married Thomas Williams. Stephen Garrett, Armstead Burt, Jeffry Sharpton, George Graves, and John Middleton to partition land among Thomas Williams in right of wife Joice, Elizabeth Thomas, James Thomas, Sarah Thomas, and William Thomas the latter being entitled to his own share as well as that of his brother John C Thomas. Commission to partition sworn 21 April 1817.

Copy of will of James Thomas 16 August 1805 by M Simkins, O.E.D. Unto Elisabeth Thomas my wife my plantations and Negroes, stock, tools, furniture during her lifetime and at her death to be equally divided amongst my children. To son John negro boy Zack, dau Joice Negro wench Tresa(?), son Silas Negro Peter, son William Negro boy Abram, son James a Negro boy Dick being Biners child, dau Elizabeth Negro girl Beck. Executors John Boyd and Bartlett Martin. /s/ James Thomas 29 November 1803. Wit Charles Olds, Ezekiah Boyd, Meredith Jeter.

Plat of land of estates of James and Elizabeth Thomas near Bull Sluice as divided, certified 25 May 1817 by John Boyd D.S.

Plat of land belonging to estate of James Thomas certifies 19 May 1817 by John Boyd D.S. shows land of Eliza Calliham crossed by road to Augusta.

Return of Commissioners Stephen Garrett, Armstead Burt, Jephrey Sharpton, Geo Graves and John Middleton, 31 May 1817. Partition confirmed by Henry W DeSaussure.

Inventory of estate of James Thomas decd, 29 March 1805.

John C Thomas of Wilkison County, Mississippi Territory, to his brother William Thomas of Edgefield, South Carolina, his undivided distributive share of estate of their father James Thomas deceased, 1 January 1816. Wit H K Boyd, John Boyd Junr, W E Boyd. /s/ John C Thomas. Proven 27 Jany 1816 by Henry K Boyd; Thos Meriwether JP. Recorded 12 Feby 1816 by M Mims.

#24   Leroy Hammond junior, Susanna Hammond, Mary Moore Rambo, Martha Scantlin Rambo, Reuben James Rambo, Matilda Elizabeth Rambo, Albert Jefferson Rambo, and Augustus Baldwin Rambo vs George Hancock, Bill. To Hon William Dobbins James, Waddy Thomson, Henry William DeSaussure & Theodore Gaillard. Susanna Hammond while sole on 13 April 1807 complained in her own name as Susanna Rambo widow of Joseph Rambo decd and also as next friend in the name of [her children named as above] against John C Allen, George Hancock admr of estate of James McQueen decd, Ann McMcQueen, Peter McQueen, Caroline McQueen & William McQueen.

Proceeding against Joseph Rambo by authority & on behalf of his landlord James McQueen, 16 November 1808 distrained the property, T. Hall, constable. Copy: promissory note signed by Joseph Rambo to James McQueen for rent of plantation at forks of road to Cherokee Ponds, one dollar rent pr week, 19 May 1807.

John C Allen, sheriff when land of Joseph Rambo was sold under an execution in favor of suit of Thos Garrett & Co and was purchased by John Hall agent of James McQueen for Susanna Rambo and her children. Hall informed me McQueen afterwards recd titles from me, telling me at the same time the land was for the benefit of Mrs Rambo & her chldren. John Hall told me the money was furnished by Mrs Rambo, but I do not recollect whether McQueen ever wrote me to that effect. He told me verbally very often the land was for benefit of Mrs Rambo & her children. I do not know what was the particular situation of Mrs. Rambo, further than that she usually had management of their house which was a public one; Rambo was usually drunk.

Other witnesses: David Barnett, John Miller, Eason C Drake.

Benjamin Grumbles in conversation with James McQueen in Campbellton in 1805 heard McQueen say (in the presence of George Grumbles) that Mrs Rambo had furnished him with part of the money to purchase the land where LeRoy Hammond now lives, that he got John Hall to make the purchase, that he would pay off the ballance of the money, that he would make her titles any time.

Isaac Hopkins said he thought James McQueen in good circumstances, did not know the value of the land. 11 June 1814. Commissioners John R Bartee, Joseph Fuller, John Tarrance.

#25 Lud Harris & wife Eliza vs J R Pointsett & Mary Ann Ramsay. John Walker in his lifetime possessed a Negro woman named Charity, made verbal gift in 178[?] and gave sd wench to his daughter Eliza. At death of her father which took place on 27 July 1788 his widow Mary Ann Walker, mother of your oratrix, married Ephraim Ramsay, one of the judges of the court of Common Pleas and into whose possession sd Negro came; sd Negro was not the property of John Walker. Ephraim Ramsay frequently said that sd Negro belonged to your oratrix and that he had no claim to her. In 1796 Dr David Ramsay, Ephraim Ramsay & Charles Goodwin purchased from the late Thomas Galphin Silver Bluff lands on Savannah River; among other things agreed to with William Greenwood, atty in fact of William Higginson surviving copartner of Higginson & Greenwood merchants, pay three thousand five hundred pounds for which George Galphin on 4 June 1792 confessed judgment and also in Georgia in May of 1794, that after the purchase afsd David Ramsay, Ephraim Ramsay and Charles Goodwin, to produce assent of William Greenwood, agreed to satisfy sd judgment and pay [complicated land difficulties in Georgia, Charleston and Edgefield] in consequence of which the sd Negroes among which were the Negro Charity and children Anney, Fanny, Adam, Clarinda, Sally, Pegg, Glasgow, Dorcas, Stephen, Joe were brought to Edgefield Court House to be sold. Lud Harris claimed the Negroes in right of his wife and forbid the sale in consequence of which Barna McKinney who had obtained assignment of sd mortgage and Christopher Fitzsimmons who attended on behalf of J R Pointsett refused to indemnify the sheriff and enforce the sale. After the mortgage of sd Negroes your orator married with your oratrix sd Eliza Walker and knew nothing of the gift by your oratrixs father untill your orator was informed of it by the late Mrs Elizabeth Eliza Goodwin, as your oratrix was not more than one or two years old when the transaction took place. The girl was always called hers and waited on your oratrix untill sd Negro had children and after her death having lost all hopes of establishing the gift as above stated your orator & oratrix did not assert the claim untill 4th July 1812 when your oratrix was accidentally informed and attended the sale on the Monday following and forbid the sale. Ephraim Ramsay departed this life on 18 November

1800 intestate leaving widow and children. Mary Ann Ramsay your oratrix's mother & Dr John Ramsay administered the estate; John Ramsay has since departed this life. J R Pointsett confederating with divers persons hath lately directed the sheriff to seize sd Negroes and sell them in November about six days from this time (30th Oct 1816) defrauding your orator & oratrix of their just rights by the improper conduct of Ephraim Ramsay. Ellison & Glascock complts sols. Lud Harris swears the above bill is true, 31 Oct 1816; /s/ Lud Harris. Notification to J R Pointsett. Notification to Sheriff, 31 Oct 1816 to stay proceedings under the mortgage of certain negroes now in sheriff's hands to be sold as property of Ephraim Ramsay decd which mortgage is now owned by R Pointsett.

#26 Taliofero Livingston, Washington Bostick, Willis Bostick and William Bostick vs Davis Bostick. Complainants were executors of will of Toliver Bostick decd. Davis Bostick's action on a note of hand purporting to have been drawn by Toliver Bostick, made payable to William Jones or bearer, and obtained judgment against estate for $450 with interest; no witness to note, it was given to Davis Bostick in consideration of Negro girl Nancy, exrs being well acquainted with actions of Toliver Bostick have no knowledge of transaction with Wm Jones or Davis Bostick except the purchase of Nancy of Davis Bostick for which Negro Toliver Bostick gave his Note to Davis Bostick, drawn in favour of Jones which note Toliver Bostick paid off. Further, Davis Bostick has produced two notes of same amount one dated 11th, the other 22d of same month and year, both notes for same amount, one of which your orators have now in their possession, same being paid off by the deceased; the other is the one which was fraud of Toliver Bostick in his lifetime both having been given for the same consideration, charging Toliver Bostick and estate of Toliver Bostick with $900 when in fact Toliver paid note for Negro girl. Sworn by Washington Bostick 19 April 1816; Whit Brooks commr.

Davis Bostick ads Exrs of Tolaver Bostick decd. Bill of costs on notice & application for an injunction. Arguments thereon & application dismissed with costs. A second notice for an application to Judge Thompson at Abbeville on amended bill for injunction. Case transferred to Equity, Washington District.

#27   74 items Jose Cunningham, guardian of William Cunningham and Catharine Cunningham minors over 14 years vs David B Thompson. John Cunningham died 8 July 1799 leaving two minor children afsd and widow Polly Cunningham, and estate amounting to $1556.66. Previous to inventory and on 14 October 1799 Polly Cunningham took out ltrs/admn, giving bond with Thomas Butler and Robert Christy as securities, sale of personal estate on 25 August 1800 $762.76 3/4. At sd sale Polly Cunningham purchased a Negro wench and four children for $500 which had been appraised at $800, among which was a boy named Isaac and a girl named Jude. Shortly afterwards 20 November 1800 Polly Cunmningham, widow, gave her children William Cunningham and Catharine Cunningham the two slaves, William the boy Isaac and Catharine the girl Jude as appears by Deed/gift recorded. In 1800 Polly Cun-ningham married David W Thompson the dft to this bill who as admr in right of his wife made returns on 29 September 1802 and other returns up to 11 December 1807 due to estate of John Cunningham [blot] besides interest. Since that period Polly Thompson has died leaving 3 or 4 children. David W Thompson's power as admr therefor ceased. He had been apptd guardian for minor children William and Catharine and gave bond with security. Sd children have been in the family of your orator for more than two years although David W Thompson has had the constant possession of the two Negroes, their property, ever since he married Polly Cunningham, except Isaac for about 3 or 4 months, has now possession of them and utterly refused to deliver them to your orators. For use and hire of sd Negroes Isaac now 18 years, Jose Cunningham feels justified in charging David W Thompson from time sd boy was 10 years of age up to present, making for 9 years the total sum of $225 besides interest, that he charges for use and hire of Negro girl Jude now 14 years only the sum of $55 Dollars besides interest. [No date] Simkins Plffs solicitor.

Jose Cunningham & Arthur Tinsley & wife agt Mark Matthews & Douglas Holloway admrs of David T Thompson. Jose Cunningham guardian of William Cunningham and late guardian of Catharine terminated by her marriage with Arthur Tinsley. David W Thompson, now deceased. On 22 June 1815 Catharine married Arthur Tinsley. Mark and Douglas, dfts, admrs on estate of David W. Thompson. Filed 12 Jany 1817. Simkins & McDuffie Plffs sols.

Douglass Holloway & Mark Matthews admrs of David W Thompson decd ads Jose Cunningham, gdn. At sale of goods and chattels of John Cunningham, Polly Cunningham, admr, being highest bidder, purchased the greater part of property. The sum being inferior to value of sd property and wishing to make provision for children afsd and to put them upon a footing with herself or nearly so, she executed deed but same was inoperative as it never was delivered, but retained in Polly's possession. She, altering her manner of making provision for sd children, obtained another order of sale of property of sd intestate, sold it at a fair price, she becoming purchaser being highest bidder, thereby making the deed afsd which altho it purports to have been exhibited at a period subsequent to the last sale, yet these defts charge that sd Deed was executed but never delivered between the periods of the first and second sales. David W Thompson by marrying Polly Cunningham had three children which are now living with dft Douglass Holloway. Polly made verbal request in her lifetime that personal property of children of John Cunningham should after her death be left under the guardianship of David W Thompson and by way of enforcing sd request she reduced same to writing not long before her death, called upon this dft with Joseph Raburn to witness same which they did. Bacon dfts solr. Sworn 3 June 1817 /s/ Douglass Holloway, /s/ Mark Matthews.

Estate accounts reported by Jose Cunningham.

David W Thompson ads Joseph Cunningham. Thompson married widow Polly Cunningham in November 1800; she died about 22 October 1810. Property of John Cunningham was sold by order of John Simkins, Ordinary, Edgefield District, about 21 April 1800; Polly Cunningham before marriage with dft bought greater part at price inferior to value of same. Wishing to make provision for the children she had by John Cunningham and to prevent any part getting into hands of relatives of Cunningham by whom she considers herself cruelly treated after the death of her Husband, she applied to this dft to write a deed to her two children for the two young Negroes mentioned. Dft here charges date of deed was altered before it was committed to record, forasmuch as it was executed about [blank] by reference to records of Edgefield District it purports to have been executed 20 November 1800, dft is confident as to this last fact from recollection of Polly Cunningham's declaration when she applied to dft to write afsd deed, to wit that as she had purchased the property afsd at reduced price, she wished to make some provision for her children, and that sd deed was executed at time afsd. Being unable to reconcile to her feelings the purchase of the property afsd at a price so inferior to its real value she took the advice of her frinds and acquaintances, and of John Simkins Esqr, Ordinary, and procured another order of sale of property which agreeably to sd order took place on 25 August 1800. Polly Cunningham about time of her death enjoined it as last request upon dft to take charge of the children afsd and to act towards them in such manner as might think most promotive of their interest; fearing a verbal request might not be obligatory upon him or operative in law, she committed same to writing which was witnessed by Mark Matthews and Joseph Raborn, and by this dft lodged in office or Ordinary but which has been lost or mislaid. Dft saith that the two Negroes contained in sd deed were at time of execution and almost ever since unproductive, that one of them at the time afsd was three years old and the other one year old, that they were contained in the family which was purchased by sd Polly Cunningham at sale afsd. Dft has not only raised the infant slaves but also raised and educated in a manner suitable to their condition in life the afsd children, and would have continued but said children were surreptitiously taken out of the house of dft without his knowledge and contrary to his desire. The Negroes with increase of the female are now worth more than the whole estate sold for. About three years ago Joseph Cunningham delivered to him a platt and grant of 350 acres in Pendleton District which was one half of 700 acres devised to John Cunningham by his father, also a note of hand devised afsd, executed by William Melton of Georgia for four guineas which remains in possession of dft uncollected as dft was never able to ascertain where in Georgia William Melton resided; a search for him would cost more than the amount of sd note. He also has a platt of 188 acres originally granted to James Cunningham and was by James Cunningham conveyed to John Cunningham, believes that afsd deed cannot pass the property thereon contained owing to reservations and restrictions thereof; it remained in possession of Polly Cunningham until 20 November 1800 when deed purported to have been [no ending to this document]

Testimony of William Partain with respect to Negroes for which hire is charged. Accounts of estate of John Cunningham deceased.

Deed of Gift, Polley Cunningham being uncertain of the time of my death when my dear children William Cunningham and Caty Cunningham may be left desolate of parents and be exposed to the uses and misfortunes of this world, it behoveth me to provide for the maintainance, support and livelihood of each of my two well beloved children afsd by a Deed of Gift of following Negroes: to son William Negro boy Isaac age three; to daughter Caty Negro girl Juda one year old, 20 November 1800. /s/ Polley (x) Cunningham. Wit Jas Lanier, Buckner (x) Thompson. Proven by James Lanier, 20 November 1800.

June Term 1818, Jose Cunningham vs David W Thompson. Counsel for dft has attempted to invaludate deed. Its execution has been satisfactorily proven. It vests property absolutely in the donees and must be carried into effect. David W Thompson carried it to the Clerks office to be recorded after his marriage with Mrs Cunningham the mother of the minors which shews that the deed was not entered into with a view of destroying his marital rights. Ordered dfts deliver to complts the Negroes in the bill mentioned amd that they do account before the commissioner for their hire since marriage of Catherine and that residue of estate of John Cunningham be distributed according to the directives of the Act abolishing the right of primogeniture and that dft pay the cost of suit out of sd estate. W Thompson.

Testimony of James Lanier regarding execution of a deed of Mrs. Polly Cunningham to her two children William and Caty Cunningham. Witness says he was a subscribing witness, that it was executed 10 or 15 days before Mrs Cunningham's marriage to Thompson. Says marriage of Mrs Cunningham and Mr Thompson took place on the 4 December. He does not know who kept the deed after its execution, but that Thompson brought it down to have it recorded. /s/ Andrew P Butler.

John Power who survived Thos Cobb and Saml Crafton, coobligors with John, to answer to John Simkins Judge of Court of Ordinary in a plea that [blank] No date.

Sale by Polly Cunningham widow of John Cunningham, 25 August 1800. Buyers: Polley Cunningham, Robert McRea, Drewry Mathews, Peter Thomson, Catherine Lanier, William Forsyth. Jno Simkins OED.

#28 10 items. Barksdale Gardner vs Elias Morgan and others. Bill for Partition filed 26 October 1818. William Morgan on 19 August 1797 conveyed to his wife Margaret Morgan and to his children Martha Morgan, Nancy Morgan, Elias Morgan, Polly Morgan, Lucy Morgan, and John Morgan his Negroes Tom, Nance, James, Aimy, and Silvey with his goods and chattels, and property to live on till his son John Morgan arrives at age 21 and then to be equally divided. Widow Margaret now dead. Barksdale Gardner married Martha Morgan who is now dead, Nancy Morgan also dead unmarried, Polly Morgan married William Kennedy who is now dead leaving widow Polly and one child William Kennedy, Lucy Morgan married Reuben Newman and is now dead leaving one child Nancy Ann Crawford Newman, John Morgan has arrived at age 21; he and Elias Morgan and Polly Kennedy have the whole of sd Property except one Negro boy named [blank] and some stock which sd Elias Morgan has illegally sold. Simkins & McDuffie, plffs sols.

#29 36 items. Benjamin Ryan vs Samuel Marsh and wife et al. No date. In late 1700s orator's uncle Benjamin Ryan Sr gave him financial help, mortgaged Negroes. Orator delivered Negroes to uncle for uncle's natural life; at his death to be returned to orator; in event of orator's death, to orator's children. Orator delivered a valuable woman Sue with her children and received a mare. Sue and increase now number fifteen, her children Silvey, Harriet, Polaski, Hannah, Milly, Moses, Thursa and Lucy; Altama, David and Henry children of Silvey; Mahala and Greenberry children of Harriet; David a boy of another family. Benjamin Ryan Sr died 11 November 1813[?] childless, leaving widow Milly Ryan extx, his brother Capt John Ryan and friend Capt Richard Johnson exrs of his will. Exrs to have Silvy, Polaski, Hannah and Milly emancipated. Disposed of the other with the rest of his estate notwithstanding he had frequently been heard to say that he only held sd Negroes during his life and that his nephew your orator Benj Ryan had absolute right of them. Negroes are in possession of Milly Marsh late Milly Ryan and her husband Samuel Marsh. /s/ Bacon, complts sol. Milly Marsh hath since died intestate and Samuel Marsh hath taken out ltrs/admn, securities Abner Blocker, Allen Addison.

Answer of Samuel Marsh to complaint of Benjamin Ryan. Marsh never heard of an agreement or mortgage between Benj Ryan and his uncle relative to Sue and her children or any other Negro which were to become property of sd Benjamin upon death of his uncle; believes such agreement existed but sees agreement in a different way. Says that before his marriage with Amelia Ryan the plf Benjamin Ryan sued Amelia before a magistrate for balance of money said to be due him by his uncle Benjamin Ryan, plf came to Amelia's house to settle with her upon which Amelia mentioned to him that she had heard he intended preferring claims against the estate of her deceased husband, upon which he said others were more to blame than him in these matters, that Amelia had been more kind in giving him money than any friend he had; Saml had the information and contract from his wife before her death.

Sworn by Saml Marsh 10 June 1817.

Answer of John Ryan surviving executor of late Benjamin Ryan decd one of defts of bill of complaint of Benjamin Ryan, filed 10 June 1817. John is ignorant of transaction between his brother and sd complainant with respect to sale and purchase of sd Negroes. Did not hear his brother say that he had sd negroes only during his life. Goodwin, Solr. Sworn 1 April 1817 by John Ryan. Chas Goodwin .

Appraisement of Benjamin Ryan's estate. Negroes Jack, Isaac, David, Gibb, Charles, Cato, Benjamin; Caty and children Peter, Benjamin, Beck and Moses; Aimy & children Lorenzo, Nero, Margaret, Mary; Harriett and child Mahaly; Sue and chlidren Moses, Thursa. Mary, Will and wife and children John, Alfred, and Sarah.
Two children Altamont and David. Girl Lucy. 9 December 1813.

Benjn Ryan vs S Marsh et ux, decree. Columbia, Dec. 1818. No proof of fraud practiced by Benjamin Ryan decd on his nephew. No understanding has been proved. Henry Wm DeSaussure, Theodore Gailiard, Thos Waites, Wm D James.

#30   25 items. Solomon Lucas vs Wm Nichols and others. Robert Roebuck died 1798 leaving a small personal estate; his father John Roebuck administered, your orator and John Hall his securities. Sd John Roebuck did not properly administer or pay to distributees of sd Robert their respective shares. John Roebuck died 1801. William Nichols, since moved to western country, administered. Robert Roebuck left five children: Winifred or Winney Roebuck since married [torn] Cannon, Elizabeth Roebuck since married to John Hardy, Mary or Polly Roebuck since married to Daniel Hardy, Black[?] Roebuck since married [torn] Day, and Benjamin Roebuck. Some distributees of Robert Roebuck have obtained judgment against your orator for $175 on 5 January 1813; execution issued. Your orator is poor and possessed of little property. No person has administered on estate of John Roebuck since William Nichols' departure; he left considerable personal estate ($687) and land; he left seven children: Robert Roebuck, Phoebe Roebuck since married to George Randall or Randolph, Ann Roebuck since married to [blank] Green, Polly Roebuck, Elizabeth Roebuck since married to William Nichols, Ezekiel Roebuck, and James Roebuck, six of whom together with the children of Robert were entitled to distribution of his estate. Ann Green and her husband have died leaving John Green, Silas Green, William Green, Bodia Green since married to Isaac Hopkins, Frances Green since married to Saunders Day. Saunders Day is now in possession of 213 acres on Horse Creek which belonged to sd John Roebuck which your orator believes would indemnify him for money he has been obliged to pay for sd John Roebuck; there is other estate property in hands of persons unknown to orator, especially a Negro man named Sam who was sold by sd James Roebuck who never administered on the estate of sd John Roebuck without any authority to sell. Ellison, complts sol.

Answers of James Day, Daniel Hardy and John Hardy to complaint of Solomon Lucas. Robert Roebuck died, complainant and John Hall were securities of John Roebuck the alleged administrator; John Roebuck died and William Nichols administered. Robert left five children of which James Day married Elizabeth, John Hardy married Clarissa, Daniel Hardy married Mary. Sworn 7 October 1816 by James Day, John Hardy, Daniel Hardy.

Answer of Sanders Day to complaint of Solomon Lucas: never received a cent of the estate of John Roebuck; purchased land from heirs of John Roebuck eight years ago. Sworn 3 June 1818; /s/ Saunders (x) Day.

GENEALOGICAL ABSTRACT OF EDGEFIELD EQUITY COURT RECORDS

Discovery 5 June 1818. Robert Roebuck died; his father John administered his estate, wasted some assets. John died. William Nichols, a son-in-law, administered his estate, distributed among his children and grandchildren their respective shares thereof except about seventy Dollars. Complainant and John Hall who is either dead or left the state were securities for his administration of John Roebuck.

15 June 1801 appraisement of estate of John Roebuck decd. Negro old woman Nan, girl Jean. /s/ John Hatcher, /s/ Isaac Kirkland, /s/ John (x) Day, /s/ James Mosley, certified 6 Feby 1813 by John Simkins, ordinary. Sales to George Randol, James Day, Ezekiel Robuck, Polley Robuck, Joseph Janes, Willm Nichols, Willm Green, Isaac Hopkins, Willm Day, Thos Swarengin, Sanders Day, Mary Swarengin.

Arbitors Christian S Breithaupt, John Curry, Hugh Ballentine. $175 to be paid by dft to plfs. 5 January 1812. Dozier, Plf atty.

Film No. JR.4069.

#31   Saml Shannon vs Danl Colvin, foreclosure of mortgage.   No date.

#26 Saml Shannon vs Danl Colvin, foreclosure of mortgage, filed 29 Jany 1818.   Samuel Shannon in 1809 was indebted to [blank] of Edgefield District $170 and Daniel Colvin and Daniel Colvin became security for payment of same; suit was brought by sd [blank] agst orator for the recovery of debt, principal interest & costs amounting to $260 paid by Daniel Colvin.   On 14 or 15 March 1809 orator to secure payment to Daniel Colvin executed conveyance to sd Daniel of 146 acres on Savannah River for $500. Only $260 was paid. Agreement between orator and Daniel was that wherever your orator should be able to pay $260 with interest, the sd conveyance should be void and land returned to orator.   On [blank] orator tendered to Daniel sd sum with interest but he refused to receive the money and to deliver the land.   Ellison & Glascock complts sols.

#32 John J Johnston vs James Johnston & others. Bill for title to land.   On 18 February 1814 James Johnston since deceased agreed to sell to orator 600 acres on South Edisto River near Cumboa's mill consisting of four surveys whereon James Johnston then resided bounded by lands of Daniel Coalter, Cumboa upon condition that orator John J Johnston should make title to 2,400 acres adj lands of sd James Johnston which he had lately purchased of Abraham Richardson, lying on Wises Creek and Big Horse Creek adj lands of Wise and Pardue. Harden Blalock who married Margaret Johnson daughter sd James Johnston took out letters of admin on James's estate.   Orator made conveyance to Harden Blalock as legal representative of James Johnson of 2500 acres. Needs heirs to make him a good title to his 600 acres on Edisto River.   Heirs of James Johnston: James Johnston junr (out of the state), Hugh Johnston, John Johnston, William Johnston (under age), and Catharine Johnston married with John Gilbreath (out of the state), Jane Johnson married James Brown which have the following children Jane Brown who married David Williamson, Catharine Brown who married John Alford,and Hathorn Hydright and wife Polly, Alexr Calhoun and Catharine Calhoun [names scratched through, interlineated, and hard to read, may not be correct. Surname also Johnson.] Margaret Johnston who married sd Harden Blalock is now dead without heirs.   Will of James Johnston proved to which Genl Joseph Hutton, Margaret Johnston and Cornelius Tobin were witnesses.   Joseph Hutton alone has qualified.   Simkins & McDuffie plffs solicitors.

Copy of original covenant, 18 February 1814. James agrees to exchange his 600 acres on Edisto near Cumboa's mill where sd Johnston lately resided and to make legal title, for 2400 acres on Horse Creek adj lands of sd James Johnston lately purchased from Abraham Richardson, and also on Wises Creek and Big Horse Creek adj lands of Capt. Wise and Purdue. /s/ James (J) Johnston, John J. Johnston. Witnesses Jos Hutton, Jno Blalock.

John J Johnston vs Genl Hutton exr of James Johnson.

John J Johnston vs James Johnston, John Johnston, James Brown, Polly Hydrac, Catharine Gilbreath, 7 June 1819.

#33 Wm Holloway vs Wm Hall. [No date] George Holloway, complainant's father, possessed considerable personal and real estate. George Holloway died 18[blank] intestate leaving ten children: James, Elizabeth, Thomas, John, Mary, Ann, George, William, Anderson, and Martha. William Hall administered estate of which your orator William Holloway was entitled to his distributive share. William Hall was appointed guardian of your orator, had in his possession the property belonging to your orator, also your orator lived with him for a considerable time during which William Hall received benefit of the labour and monies for which he has not yet accounted. Orator now age 21 and is desirous of having in his possession the property to which he is entitled. He has applied to William to come to settlement but William intends to deprive him of his rights. W Ellison, complts sol.

Bill for discovery filed 29 Jany 1818.

#34 Executors of John Hammond vs Charles Goodwin and admrs of LeRoy Hammond. Filed 5 Feby 1818. Charles Hammond and Stephen Garrett executors of John Hammond decd obtained judgment against Charles Goodwin and Leroy Hammond 19 November 1804 for $185.75 with interest from 20 July 1802 and $12.31 1/4 for costs. Sd judgment has never been satisfied nor any part of it paid. Sd Charles Goodwin has become insolvent; William Garrett and Sarah Q Hammond are the legal representatives of sd Leroy Hammond. Asks that afsd sums be paid. Simkins & McDuffie compts sols.

#35 Thomas Branson and wife Mary vs William Holliday and others. Partition relief. Filed 6 January 1818. William Holliday Senr died intestate seized of about 700 acres. William Holladay left seven children: William, James, Elenor who married Eli Branson, Peggy married Samuel Bell, Lydia married Bennett McMillan, oratrix married with orator, and Anna who has until very lately been a minor, being at present about age 22. Orator and oratrix state that they are entitled to one seventh part of two thirds of sd land as heirs of William Holladay decd, they also state that William Holladay left widow Sarah Holladay who was entitled to one third part of the land. Widow Sarah died during summer of 1817, orator & oratrix became entitled to one seventh part of her third of land afsd; so your orator and oratrix are now entitled to one seventh part of whole tract. William Holladay together with his mother Sarah Holliday admrd on personal estate of sd William Holladay decd and misconceiving or disregarding their functions retained possession of afsd tract for years without rendering any account of rents and profits. Believe William Holliday has sold to James Holladay, Pearson Holloway, Douglass Holloway, John Ramsay, and Samuel Bell the afsd tract or parts thereof which pretended purchasers are now in possession of said land and liable to account to orator and oratrix for their distributive share of the rents and profits. The afsd land is worth Six thousand Dollars. Annual rents and profits are of considerable value. Asks that sd William Holladay, James Holladay, Pierson Holloway, Douglas Holloway, John Ramsay, Samuel Bell make separate answers on oath. Chas Mayson, comps sols.

#36. A B Addison and wife vs Nancy Butler and others. Bill for partition. [10 items] Filed Jun 1818. Allen B Addison and Patience Addison were guardians of Nancy Butler, John R Butler, Elizabeth S Butler, and William M Butler. Stanmore Butler died seized of several tracts and a lot in Edgefield Village; one tract on Cuffeetown Creek of 236 acres adj lands of [page torn], Stephens Creek containing 187 acres adj lands of Mrs P Gouedy and James Allen, 175 acres adj Sampson Butler, and lot in village of Edgefield adj Peter Labord's lot. Two tracts are entirely unproductive. It is to interest of all parties that afsd land and lots be sold.

Answer of Nancy Butler, Jno R Butler, Elizabeth S Butler, William M Butler, to the Bill of Allen R Addison an wife Patience. Defendants being minors and not capable of judging own interests submit it to Court to determine. Whitfield Brooks, guardian

A. B. Addison

175 acres in Village of Edgefield sold to A B Addison.
187 acres on Stephens Creek adj Mrs Gouedy sold to George[?] Butler.
236 acres on Cuffeetown Creek adj Geo Shelnut sold to G McDuffie.
House & lot in village of Edgefield sold to Y S Brooks

Exrs of Prior

2482 acres Town Creek sold to John Sturzenegger.
1000 acres sold to John Sturzenegger

Jos Jennings

100 acres on Catfish Creek sold to James Hix

Wm Garrett

Negro fellow Lowden sold to Stephen Garrett

Petition for sale of land, 4 June 1818, "sale of the property contemplated in the bill will result to the benefit of the chldren." /s/ Whit Brooks, commr in Equity.

#37 Henry Chaucer Ashton vs Lewis Cantelou and others, Bill for injunction and relief. Joseph Ashton, adoptive father of your orator died leaving will "I do give and bequeath all my estate and property real and personl of every description unto my true and loving wife Lucy Ashton and for her use during her natural life and at her decease the whole thereof to devolve on my adopted son Henry Chaucer Ashton." [torn] 799 ½ acres. Widow Lucy married Charles Stovall who became executor in right of his wife, sold the land under an execution against the estate notwithstanding there was sufficiency of personal property for the payment of debts. Your orator, then a minor, sd land was purchased by Ratcliff in 1812, conveyed by Ratcliff to Lewis Cantelou. Claims fraud by Stovall. Simkins & McDuffie, solicitors for plf.

Order by Henry Wm DeSaussure, Columbia, 26 Sept 1817, that Lewis Cantelou, Charles Stovall, and Richard Radcliff be enjoyned from committing waste on the premises and particularly from cutting timber and clearing sd land until further order of the Court.

Answer of Louis Cantelou to complaint of Henry Chauser Ashton. Is ignorant of testamentary legal disposition or any codicils to Joseph Ashton's will. Dft admits he was once shown a purported will of Joseph Ashton, same was worn and defaced but whether it was genuine will of Joseph Ashton and whether same remained unrevoked he cannot say. Goodwin

& Bacon, complts Solrs. /s/ L Cantelou. Sworn 27 Novr 1817, A. Edmunds JP.

Henry C Ashton vs Lewis Cantelou. Decree. Dft purchased land for valuable consideration without knowledge of complainants claim if he has any, no restraint upon the privileges Cantelou has a right to exercise on his own property. W Thompson. Feby 4, 1818.

#38 Joel Hill ads Elijah Lyon. Bill for injunction & relief. [31 items] Defendant sold land to plaintiff, warranting it to contain 247 acres which he then believed to be true quantity, upon a resurvey by John Lyon and John Blocker Esqrs it measured only 217 ½ acres. Purchase money was $1580; first payment was Negro fellow at high price of $600 and about $25 cash. Plaintiff gave note for $150 payable in a month but did not pay for a year. Balance due 16 February 1810 on which note dft has never received one cent. Plaintiff on land over six years and has mortgaged it to the Bank of the State of South Carolina. Dft sued plaintiff, judgment March Term last; sheriff levied on Negro fellow, five horses of no great value, and land. Dft committed blunder of entering into arbitration bond. 31 August 1815. /s/ Elijah Lyon.

Joel Hill complains that 16 Feruary 1809 he purchased land of Elijah Lyon [facts as above]. Removed from Georgia and settled on the land. Arbitrament and Award of David Crawford and others, on 16 June last, awarded to orator $334.75. Asks that sheriff be ordered to desist from intended sale of of property levied on. Sworn 25 July 1815. /s/ Joel Hill.

Columbia, July 28[?], 1815 order injunction issued restraining dft from proceeding against complainant upon his giving security for payment of amount of judgment and costs. Henry Wm DeSaussure.

Copy of deed, Elijah Lyon to Joel Hill, 16 February 1809, land on Hardlabor of Stephens Creek. Witnesses William Price Jr, Jesse Hill. Dower release by Polly (~) Lyon. Proved by William Price 16 February 1809. Plat shows 247 acres adj lands of William Price, Joseph Wallace, Geo Harris, Hardlabor, Stephens, and Cuffeetown Creeks.

Arbitration bond 16 June 1815 signed by David Crawford, Garret Freeman, John Longmire, Richd Quarles, Pleasant Thurmond.

Plat 25 September 1812 shows 217 acres on Hardlabor, Cuffeetown and Stevens Creeks adjoining lands of James Quarles.

#39 Joel Hill vs Anderson Turpin and Samuel Williams. Bill for Relief. Verbal agreement to erect buildings at Mount Enon in Georgia. Anderson Turpin absconded, was arrested, and jailed in Georgia. Samuel Williams proceded no further with work. Plf paid Williams amount due him. 7 August 1809 signed agreement with Mr Turpin and S Williams, $199 due Turpin. Turpin left neighborhood before final settlement. Anderson Turpin was indebted to orator $501.23 3/4 besides sum of [blank] on two notes.

Answer of Anderson Turpin. Hill owes him money, doesn't know how memorandum came into hands of Mssrs Bacon & Martin for collection, is ready to fulfill contract. /s/ Anderson (x) Turpin. Wit Jos. Eastland. Sworn 27 May 1816.

Joel Hill placed in hands of John S Glascock two notes of Anderson Turpin that he has not been able to collect. 19 Feb 1816. /s/ Joel Hill.

Decree. Complainant to pay cost of suit. W Thompson.

#40 Robert Walker et al vs John Walker, bill for partition. Filed 4 Feby 1819. Robert Walker's father, Joseph R Walker, died possessed of land on road from Edgefield Court

House to Abbeville, as yet undivided; left a widow now deceased and twelve children.

Answer of John Walker, minor, by his guardian Beverly Samuel.

Bill for partition. John S Jeter, complts solr, asks that Whit Brooks be apptd guardian ad litem for Francis Walker and Geo Walker dfts and minor children.

Commr Whit Brooks reports that James Beams, Jeremiah Hatcher and Matthew Mims examined the land; it is impracticable to divide; interests of all parties promoted by sale of land, 4 Feby 1819.

No.JR.4069. Files 31-40

#41 Steven Wilson, wife Elizabeth P Wilson & Wm Prior otherwise called William Prior Grubs vs John Prior & others. Bill for relief. Filed 10 Feb 1818. (41 items) John Prior died in 1797 leaving will by which William is entitled in his own right and Steven in right of his wife, each to one fifth part of real and personal estate of John Prior decd. Left 3482 acres on Town Creek. Executors sold sd land to Charles Goodwin for $4285.71; took bond and mortgage of Chas Goodwin and LeRoy Hammond. John Prior decd, apptd John Starr, Jacob Zinn Senr and his son John Prior now decd executors. They refuse to settle with Wm Prior, have partially settled with Steven Wilson and Elizabeth his wife, refuse to pay interest on amount due them. LeRoy Hammond has died; Sarah Q Hammond and William Garrett admrs on his estate. John Prior exr has also died and Sarah Prior and Andrew Butler are apptd exrs and qualified. Asks that Charles Goodwin, and admrs of LeRoy Hammond, and John Starr, Jacob Zinn Senr and exrs of John Prior make true answers on oath.

Stephen Wilson & wife vs Exrs of John Prior. Report, May 1819. Exrs are indebted to Stephen Wilson in right of his wife in sum $2082.59 and to Wm Prior Grubs $3128.48, Whit Brooks, commr, 26 May 1819.

Charles Goodwin ads Major Jacob Zinn and John Starr surviving Exrs of John Prior. Answer & disclaimer. Feby 1818. John Prior Junr sold to James Otis Prentis. John Prior died afterwards but no titles made, contract rescinded; Goodwin purchased the property and gave bond and mortgage. At that time he was receiving an annual resource from England which soon failed, he was not able to comply with conditions of bond and mortgage. While in possession he built a grist mill, gin house, saw mill. He wanted late Col. Hammond exonerated. Sworn 2 Feb 1818. /s/ Chas Goodwin.

Answer of Sarah Prior and Andrew Butler admr and admx of John Prior Jr decd. Will of John Prior senior directs his property be divided equally among his son John who was a legitimate child and his illegitimate children Susanna Prior Grubs, Tobias Prior Grubs, Elizabeth Prior Grubs, William Prior Grubs children of Eve Grubs with whom John Prior lived at time of his death and for a long time before in a state of adultery having a lawful wife still living in England. Act of Assembly prohibits inhabitants from giving to any bastard child or woman with whom he lives in adultery any gift, legacy, or more than one fourth part of real and personal estate. By law sd Susanna P Grubs, Tobias P Grubs, Elizabeth P Grubs, and William P Grubs were not entitled to more than one fourth part of estate. Dfts wish mortgage foreclosed. Sworn by Andrew Butler. 16 January 1819.

Answer of Chas Goodwin sworn. Answer of Charles Ramsay sworn 2 July 1819 before William Nibbs JQ.

Names appearing in estate accounts: John E Anderson, George Walker, Melines C Levensworth, Eve Grubs, Edward Rowell, Jas Reid, Rd Tutt, James Alger of Savannah,

GENEALOGICAL ABSTRACT OF EDGEFIELD EQUITY COURT RECORDS

James O Prentis, Johnathan Myer, Lud Harris, Abraham Ardis, Walter Taylor, Gasper Nail, Charles Ramsay, Willliam Stewart, John Murray, Ephraim Ramsay Esqr.Nathan Miller, Joseph Wood, Nebuchadnezar Currie, Andrew Butler, John Glover, James Welch, James Fox, Hodge Holmes, Lewis Harris, John Taylor, John Lowe, Ann Zubly, John Jones, William Shinholster, George Wallow, Cradock Burnell, Charles Carter

Receipt of Elizabeth Prior $428.46 owed me from our father's estate, 8 January 1816; /s/ Elizabeth Prior.

#42 Henry Zinn agt James C Gardiner, Mary Gardiner, Dawson Atkison, Agnes Atkison. Revivor, filed 28 July 1818. [23 items] Henry Zinn of Beach Island, planter, in May 1817, filed bill against Jacob Zinn his elder brother wherein he charged that their father Valentine Zinn possessed several tracts of land on one of which near Fort Moore Bluff he resided. In November 1790 he made his will in presence of three wintesses; he died in 1791 without revoking his will. He bequeathed to his son Henry Zinn all his lands, horses, and waggons, also three Negro boys named Dick, Jack and Jim. He appointed his wife Elizabeth extx and Henry extr; however he gave his wife his property during widowhood. She married again in 17[blank]. Upon the death of his mother dft Jacob Zinn took possession of house and lands that their father devised to complainant and remained in possession thereof. Sd will was kept from Henry by his mother nor hath he ever had opportunity of proving same though he made several attempts to do so during his mother's life, the day after whose death sd will was purposedly destroyed. William Stewart is an aged man and together with several witnesses is resident out of state; there are witnesses resident in this state whose testimony may also be of service to him in establishment of sd will in Court. He asks for establishment of same.

Complainant states that Jacob Zinn received a commission to examine Alexander Downer an aged and crippled witness resident in this state in order to have his testimony perpetuated., commission executed and remains unpublished in commissioners office. Likewise obtained commission to examine William Stewart resident in Georgia a witness who prepared will for execution by sd testator but who unfortunately died before it was executed. Suit abated by death of Jacob Zinn who died intestate leaving only two daughters: Mary named to James Cotton Gardiner and Agnes married to Dawson Atkinson. James Cotton Gardiner hath obtained ltrs/admn on his father in law's estate in right of his wife Mary and they and Dawson Atkinson and his wife have possessionn of whole of sd lands.

Will of Valentine Zinn. To wife Elizabeth during her natural life if she remains a widow all my estate, if she marries, only her necessary part. To son Jacob Zinn Negro man Jacob, also what is due me as per account enclosed amounting to forty pounds. To son Henry Zinn all my lands, horses, waggons, Negro boys Dick, Jack, Jim. Daughter Elizabeth Malone and Elizabeth A. Malone Negro woman Doll. To daughter Margaret Baker Negro man named Scippio, women Jenny and Selah. To dau Catharine Pasery(?) Negro worth forty pounds which son Henry is to purchase. To dau Sarah Zinn two Negroes, girl Lucy and boy Jeffery. Plantation livestock and tools at wife's death unto my children: Jacob, Henry, Elizabeth and Elizabeth A Malone her daughter, Margaret Baker, Catherine Panary(?) and Sarah Zinn. Daughters Margaret Baker and Sarah Zinn to be maintained out of estate while they remain unmarried or untill they receive their portions. Widow Elizabeth extx, son Henry Zinn extr. /s/ Valentine Zinn. Wit: James (x) Malone, /s/ Margaret (x) Baker, /s/ William Stewart.

Commission to examine witnesses in Mississippi State, filed 7 Sept 1818, taken out of the office 17 September 1818. Execution signed by John McRae, Asa Hartfield, Jacob Carter. To Doctor Thomas S Mills, John Sturzenegger, Gasper Neale Senr and Captn John Clarke Jr. Instructions to commissioners at Suit of Henry Zinn plf and Jacob Zinn Senior dft, commission to examine witnesses. Goodwin & Bacon, Sols. Whit Brooks.

Deposition of Margaret Wilson formerly Margaret Baker resident on Leaf River, Mississippi, witness aged 55, at Greene Courthouse 5 April 1819. Saw will of her father Valentine Zinn twice. Night after father Valentine Zinn died mother of her own accord in presence of myself, John Witlow, James Malone, Elizabeth Malone his wife and sister Sarah Zinn broke open paper in which will was sealed; first part of will was read by John Willson; latter part was not read. Contents of will was as follows, Negro man Jacob was left to my brother Jacob Zinn plus forty pounds, all father's lands left to Henry Zinn, two waggons and teams three Negro boys Dick, Jack & Jim, an equal share of stock and plantation tools to Henry Zinn, to Elizabeth Malone Negro girl Doll, also equal share of stock and furnitures, to Margaret Willson, myself, Negroes Scipio, Jane, and Sela and equal share of furniture and stock, to Catherine Pavny forty pounds to buy her a Negro which was to be made up out of the estate, and an equal share of stock and furniture. To my sister Sarah Zinn was left two negroes Lucy and Jeffry, also equal share of the furniture and stock. Reason for recounting contents of will was that property was not disposed of as father wished; also that I knew the original will was destroyed. I heard my father tell my mother when lying on his death bed a few days previous to his death not to let Jacob Zinn have any privilege on the plantation, that if she died he would cheat and defraud the children out of every thing. That Jacob Zinn took possession of the property and has kept it ever since. /s/ Margaret (x) Willson, 5 April 1819. /s/ John McRae, /s/ Asa Hartfield, /s/ Jacob Carter, commissioners.

June 1819. It is ordered and decreed that the complainants bill be dismissed; and that each party shall pay his own costs. Henry W DeSaussure.

#43 Henry Zinn agst Jacob Zinn Sr. Bill for discovery & relief and to perpetuate testimony. Complainant's father Valentine Zinn formerly of Beach Island made his will in 179[blank]in presence of three witnesses; in 1791 Valentine departed this life. Amongst items in sd will he bequeathed all his lands, horses and waggons and Dick, Jack and Jim to Henry Zinn. All bequeathed to wife Elizabeth during her life. After Elizabeth's death the elder brother Jacob Zinn took possession of the house and land. [repetition of foregoing material].

Answer of Jacob Zinn Sr. Father died in March or April 1791. At father's death Jacob possessed of about half of upland which father had marked off for him about 1780 and considerable portion of lowland marked off about 1784 which he received and improved confident his father would make titles as he promised. He knew nothing of execution or contents of father's will. At the death of his mother early in 1793 he took possession of that part of his father's estate which he had not previously obtained by gift of his father and has remained in constant possession, believes his mother was opposed to the establishment of the alleged will stating as the ground of her opposition that she did not believe it to be the will of her deceased husband. /s/ Jacob Zinn. 3 Feby 1818; Whit Brooks commr.

Jacob Zinn Sr ads Henry Zinn, Feb 1818. Answer of James C Gardner in behalf of self & wife & Dawson Atkison in behalf of himself & wife to bill of Henry Zinn. He knew nothing of the destruction of the will of Valentine Zinn. /s/ James C Gardner, sworn 12 Jany 1819; Whit Brooks Commr.

John Ardis vs Nathl Howell and others, 1 July 1818. Recd of Cradock Burnell Esqr of David Ardis, $3832. 67 ½ cents in full, 28 Jy[?] 1819. J Hatcher sheriff. Sheriff levied on estate of Nathaniel Howell for money owed John.

Henry Zinn vs Jacob Zinn Sr,complainant Henry Zinn give security before next court. Henry Zinn agt Jacob Zinn Sr, witnesses. Comrs names: John Sturzenegger Esq, Dr T S Mills, Gasper Neal, John C Carkin Jr. Filed 26 Septr 1817. Certified by Thos S Mills, John Sturzenegger.

Henry Zinn agt Jacob Zinn Sr. Interrogations to be administered; commissioners John Sturzenegger Esq, Dr. Thos J Mills. Deposition of Alexr Downer. Saw Elizabeth Zinn widow of Val Zinn hand paper purporting to be will of V Zinn to Judge Arthur Simkins Esqr who after looking over it handed it to [blank] Anderson Esqr the other judge who handed it back to Simkins who returned it to Elizabeth Zinn who observed that he would not or could not have anything to do with it. Henry Zinn requested court not to return sd will to Elizabeth Zinn untill he could have opportunity of proving it. /s/ Alexr Downer.

#44   Geo E Kaddell vs Chas Hammond et al. [111 items] George Eveleigh Kiddell of Bristol, Great Britain. John Hammond of Campbellton had commercial transactions and obligation with interest 1792 [faded, torn, and dark, name of Isaac Teasdale, Charles Hammond, Samuel Hammond sons of John Hammond, Messrs Johnston & Robertson of Savannah are visible].

[torn document mentions David Ramsay treasurer of South Carolina, Daniel Bird]

Geo Eveleigh Keddell vs Chas Hammond, Stephen Garrett, Samuel Hammond Junior. Complainant not entitled to an answer because he is an alien in Great Britain under allegiance to the King an enemy to this state. Goodwin, solrs. Sworn by Alexander Edmunds Esqr, Captain Charles Hammond and Stephen Garrett, 17 May 1814. Report 1819. Accounts between the parties inspected by Whit Brooks commr.

Geo E Keddell vs Chs Hammond, Report 1819. Report of estate of John Hammond decd in hands of Charles Hammond & Stephen Garrett executors, Amt of sale 19 Jany 1801, accounts to 1815, submitted 3 Jan 1819 by Whit Brooks commr.

George E Kiddell vs Exors J Hammmond. Complainant offered acknowledgment from John Hammond & Isaac Teasdale in evidence. 2 June 1817.

Plea of Charles Hammond and Stephen Garrett, exors of John Hammond. 21 May 1816. Demurrer. Isaac Teasdale now deceased, will: Elizabeth his wife now dead and [blank] his daughter extx. Daughter married James Matthews.

Answer of Charles Hammond, had conversation with his father whose new house was maliciously burned, father did not expect to live long, father expected to be murdered and wished to make Charles acquainted with his affairs, circumstances under which agreement was signed in home of Isaac Teasdale in Charleston, his horses were in Teasdale's stable under lock and key, was pressed to sign agreement, either sign or go to jail, could not have his horses and leave town. Sworn 29 March 1816, /s/ Charles Hammond.

Panton Leslie & Co, to Isaac Teasdale, Charleston, from St Augustine E F, 12 April 1797. Don Juan Fernandez has made partial payments, ballance is still due. Remits by bearer Capt Isaac Wickes $254. Accounts enclosed.

Answer of Stephen Garrett to George Eveleigh Kiddle sworn 1 June 1816.

GENEALOGICAL ABSTRACT OF EDGEFIELD EQUITY COURT RECORDS

Accounts show names of F Pardue, R Rozen, Thos Butler, Thos C Russel, James McQueen, W B Bland, D Mazake. W Shaw statement dated 23 March 1796 written in case of his death states he was present with Isaac Teasdale of Charleston and John Hammond of Campbellton at house of Mr Teasdale when settlement of accounts for some years took place; terms of agreement.

George E Kiddle vs Charles Hammond & Stephen Garrett, exors of J Hammond: Judgment of Henry Wm Desaussure, Theodore Gaillard, William D James, April 1819. Certified a true copy by Thos F Willisson, May 15, 1819.

George E Kiddell v Chas Hammond. Appeal, Judgment June 1824. /s/ Henry W Desaussure.

#45   Mary Ferguson vs Nelson F Ferguson, Bill for partition. [8 items] James Freeman, Isaac Hawes, John Ferguson and Peter Smith appraisers on 26 August valued lot No. 1 of 90 acres, laid out for Mary Ferguson widow of Eleazar, Lot #2 of 35 laid out for Nelson Ferguson son of Eleazer Ferguson decd, #3 98 acres laid out for Nelson F Ferguson. Plat shows adj lands of Patrick Spicer, James Newbey, John Barker, Enshow. 20 August 1817, Edwd Collier D.S. Plea states land bounded by Enoch Owens, James Newby, Potter. Also had three Negroes Paddy, Sylias, & Isaac on September [blank] 1816 when he died intestate leaving Mary Ferguson his widow and Nelson F Ferguson an infant under age 21 his heirs. Mary entitled to one third, Nelson to two thirds thereof. Wm Ellison complainants solicitor.

Answer of Nelson F Ferguson, has no objection to complaints bill. Thomas Ferguson guardian to Nelson F Ferguson, 3 June 1817; /s/ Thos Ferguyson(sic).

Writ of partition, directs James Freeman and Isaac Hughs chosen by complainant and John Ferguson Sr apptd by court and Peter Smith sr and John Glover chosen by guardian of dft to make partition.

#46   Melines Conckling Leavensworth, planter, agt Henry Thomas of Augusta, Georgia, merchant, et al. [12 items] relief and injunction. About 1803 Orator, had transactions with Thomas. 12 June 1806 gave note for balance due. Henry Thomas took into partnership his brother Ralph Thomas, partial liquidation of transactions between them, balance of $1900 due by orator; orator gave note for same dated 12 May 1813 on which a suit was initiated and judgment returned against orator, execution hath been lodged in sheriff's office and property of orator levied upon, property now advertized for sale next race day. Asks subpoena issue agt James Thomas and Ralph Thomas, grant writ of injunction against further proceedings. Sworn 9 August 1815 by Melines C Leavensworth; M Mims CCP.   Accounts.

#47   John Lipscomb and Sarah his wife vs Sophia Bonham & Others. Partition. To David Richardson, Presly Bland, John Mobley, Mumford Perryman and Lodowick Hill. John Lipscomb and Sarah Mary Lipscomb his wife represent that James Bonham left a widow Mrs Sophia Bonham and eight children his legitimate heirs to wit John Whit Bonham, Simeon Smith Bonham, Malicha Bonham, James Butler Bonham, Elizabeth Jemima Bonham, Rachel Juliana Bonham, Millie Lucke Bonham and Sarah Marey Lipscomb wife of sd John, all minors under age of 21, and also seized of land on Red Bank Creek of Little Saluda River, comprised of two tracts one of 500 acres originally granted to Thomas Deloach the elder by William Bull Esqr on 31 August 1774, the other granted to S Etheredge of 139 acres was conveyed by Wm Burdett to Wm H Lewis 4 September 1807; by him to James Bonham 29 Decr 1813. Also 75 acres on Red Bank Creek being part of 400 acres granted by Wm Bull to Thomas Deloach the elder 31 August 1774, conveyed by Thomas Deloach to Jesse Journagin, by Jesse to Asa Journagin, by him to James Bonham on 13 December 1808; also 115 acres on Little Salua adj lands of James Vaughn, Henry King, William Blundell, sd James Bonham, conveyed by Ross Ozborne to him 24 October 1803; of all sd tracts Sophia Bonham relict of James Bonham claims one third, and petitioners John Lipscomb and Sarah his wife claim one undivided eighth of the remaining two thirds, and whereas each of minor children and heirs of James Bonham represented by guardians legally appointed to appear February 1816 to show cause if and why a writ should not be granted to certain persons to lay out to John Lipscomb and wife Sarah Mary daughter of James Bonham one eighth of two thirds of sd land. David Richardson, Presly Bland, John Mobley, Mumford Perryman and Lodowick Hill to value the land and partition between Sophia Bonham widow and John Whitiel Bonham, Simeon Smith, Malichi, James Butler, Elizabeth Jemima, Rachel Julian, Milldge L Bondham and John Lipscomb and wife Sarah M the legatees of sd James decd. James Bonham also left 500 acres granted to John Barnet 11 February 1762 between the seashore and Broad path from the lower ferry on Santee to Hobcan ferry opposite to Charleston in Saint James Parish Santee in Craven County adj lands of John Gaillard at time of survey; also 500 acres in St Bartholomew Parish adj lands late property of Doctor Spence, by Ponpon river and by lands of late Thomas Middleton, conveyed by Benjamin Postell to sd James Bonham 1 February 1797. Sophia Bonham renounces right of dower to last two tracts. Whit Brooks Esqr, commissioner in Equity, Simkins & McDuffie Plffs sol. P Bland, Mumford Perryman, John Mobley sworn 1 June 1816.

Film No. JR.4070 Columbia, 7 Novr 1816 Henry W Desaussure. Order for sale of lands of estate of late James Bonham heretofore made by the Court of Equity to be extended to 23d of present month, giving public notice. Bond of Mrs Bonham & titles to two tracts of land.

#48   James Smyly vs David Richardson, Charlotte Strother & others, Bill, title to land. [9 items] Orator on 5 Sept 1815 purchased of George F(sic) Strother late of Edgefield 436 acres on Little Stephens Creek adj tracts owned by William [too dark to read], Little Stephens Creek Meeting House being lands on which your orator now resides, for $2200 to be paid in three instalments, $1200 on 1 January 1817, and in two equal annual instalments. When purchase was completed sd George F Strothers gave orator a bond and agreed to [fold of paper] titles to sd lands, he died leaving widow Charlotte Strother and three children George Strother, David Strother and William Strother under age of twenty one entitled to his estate. Charlotte Strother and David Richardson administed estate. Asks titles be made.
      Answer of David Richardson, Charlotte Strother admr & admx estate of George J Strother and as guardian of George, David, and William; admit land sold; admit James Smiley paid $100 as part of first installment, later received of James Smiley Eleven hundred Dollars the balance of the first installment; ask contract be fulfilled. /s/ David Richardson, /s/ Charlotte Strother, 2 June 1817. Bond of George J Strother 5 September 1816, witness Samuel Smyly, Levi Bledsoe. J S Jeter appoints David Richardson guardian for George Strother, David Strother &Wm Strother under age 21. No legal conveyance can be made by reason of the minority George J Strother's children. Commr in Equity ordered to make

titles conveying sd land to James Smyley with payment of balance due, being $1000, the minor children to have six months after their respectively attaining age 21 to shew cause against this decree. Henry W DeSaussure.

#49   James Spratt vs Martha Spratt & others, Bill for partition, 7 June 1817. James Spratt's brother John Spratt died seized of 500 acres on Pacolet River, Spartanburgh District formerly Craven County adj lands granted to Joseph Hutchins, Martha Sidy[?]. John Spratt died intestate leaving your orator; the widow of Thomas Spratt, a brother of the intestate; Martha Spratt and her eight children Margaret, Mary, John, Sally, James, Mandy, Alexander, Elizabeth; also a sister Rachel Spratt entitled to distributive shares of sd land. Martha Spratt, her children and Rachel Spratt refuse to partition of land. Asks partition be compelled.
         Rachel Spratt, Martha Spratt admx of Thomas Spratt decd and her children summoned to appear. Edgefield Sheriff J Hatcher certifies 22 May 1817 writ was delivered by deputy Mark McHowe[?].

#50   Mary Snead & others vs Jane Cobb & others, filed 18 December 1817. [no papers]

Film No.Jr.4070 Roll ED114
#51 Jeanne L Kerblay vs Christ[n] Breithaupt & others. Bill of Complaint. [83 items] To Judges William James, Waddy Thomson, Henry William Desaussure, Theodore Gaillard. & Thomas Waties. [discoloration of this right margin has caused loss of words which can probably be read in the original but not on microfilm. Handwriting makes name Mauboix/Muepois/etc illegible] Jeanne Odette Marie de Levis Mauboir widow of Joseph Marie Lequinio Kerblay and commonly known by the name of Jeanne Lequino Kerblay, is daughter of Louis Marie Francois Gaston de Levis Muibois and of Catharine Agnes de Levis Chateau Morand his wife and was entitled to her distributive share of the immense possessions of her father, of her grandfather the Marshall de Marebois and of separate estate of her mother Catharine Agnes de Levis Chateau Morand, that the fortunes of family one of the most considerable in France received fatal shock from French Revolution and near relations suffered on the scaffold. That ancestral properties were seized by national authorities and her family nearly reduced to poverty [fold of page has obliterated words] establishment of a more settled order of things...to procure partial restoration of property. Mr Guy Casimer Adelaide de Levis Muebros brother of your oratrix and Madame de Polastron her sister who were considered as emigrants and Dame Alexandrine Marie Julie Felicite de Montboisier commonly called Madame de Muepois widow of Charles Chibut Marie Gaston de Levis Muepois the other brother of your oratrix as guardian of her minor children Madame Henriette Charlotte de Levis, Therese Gabrielle de Levis wife of Louis Sylvester de Brugy Marsillac sister of your oratrix and your oratrix, worth forty nine thousand six hundred and thirty one livres. Your oratrix afterward married Joseph Marie Lequino Kerblay. Marriage contract was executed between them 1801. Your oratrix brought with her all that she might be entitled to during coverture, entirely absolved from debts of the marriage; a community of goods established between them to consist of property hereinafter named. Lequino Kerblay about 1806 removed to this state and became a naturalized citizen and purchased property from funds belonging to your oratrix; titles were made in his name whereby property became liable to distribution among his representatives. A large share of the original funds of your oratrix was expended;

and without children leaving estate purchased with funds of your oratrix. Christian Breithaupt his administrator. Oratrix further shows that after death of her husband she was deceived by Isaac D'Arnielle and married him when he had other wives living and particularly one in Virginia; your oratrix believed him to be a clergyman; he sold lands belonging to your oratrix to Walter Leigh of Georgia which sale is void. Believes Lequino Kerblay has a brother in France at Sarzeau[Savizale?] in Morbihan and also a lady named Madame Kellen whose maiden name was Lequinio the niece of sd Lequinio Kerblay. Oratrix is apprehensive that relations of her husband may claim his property. Asks for absolute possession and control of sd property but Breithaupt refuses to do so without Court's decree. Complainant seeks benefit of the marriage contract providing community of goods and property which each possessed at time of marriage and all they might afterwards acquire.

Walter Leigh ads Jeanne L Kerblay. Lequino Kerblay had among other tracts of land 398 acres on Savannah River opposite Augusta. She married I. Anselm D'arnielle, sold afsd land and paid off mortgage on negroes of Lequinio Kerblay. Title is confirmed by this court. Sworn 7 Feb 1818 by Walter Leigh.

1806 April 1 and later financial records of Lequinio Kerblay. Answer of Christian Breithaupt to bill of complaint, 2 June 1815. Commission to witnesses Polly Ballinger, Hugh Ballinger of Virginia, 15 July 1814. Deposition of James Woods taken at the tavern of Richard Burch in Livingston, Nelson County, 23 September 1816. Was acquainted with Isaac Darnielle, Amherst County, Virginia, about 1788 and afterwards, understood he had lived in Kentucky, was Episcopalian preacher, married to Elizabeth Digges and had some children, also practiced law, moved to Richmond. Mistress Elizabeth Darnielle is still living.

Deposition of Edward Harris 23 September 1816, knew Isaac Darnielle of Amherst County, present when he was married to Elizabeth Digges by Charles Crawford, had three children, moved to Richmond. Wife Elizabeth Darnielle is living in Albemarle County, Virginia. Commissioners taking depositions: Ro J Kinnard, Lee W Harris. Deposition of William H Digges taken at Richard Burch's tavern, Nelson County, VA, 23 September 1816. Was acquainted with Isaac Darnielle; he married my sister Elizabeth Digges about 1789; my sister is still living; he was pursued to Winchester by creditors; my sister returned to Amherst; about 1794 he left; Digges saw several letters written to the wife from Kentucky, Mississippi Territory, Georgia, and Carolina. Deposition of James A Lafitte. Understood Mrs Kerblay was to have all his property after his death. Heard Mr & Mrs Kerblay say that deeds of partition had been executed between the brothers and sisters of Madam Kerblay in France for that part of their Father and Mothers estate which had not been seized by the government, done before Mr Kerblay left France; money was managed by Mr Denonvilliers in Paris. Mr Kerblay told his nephew not to come to this country because he had nothing to give him, the whole of the property being the property of his wife and not his. Translation into English of the contract of future husband and intended wife.

#52   John Little guardian of Solomon Lewis Pope and Sarah Little vs John Pope exr of Solomon Pope decd, and James Robb admr of estate of Patience Rabb[Robb?] for relief. [76 items] John Little as guardian in right of his wife of Solomon Lewis Pope an infant under age of 21 and as representative of the right of his wife and your orator Sarah Little. Solomon Pope about 1774 left twelve children, four of whom were married at the time of his death, Mary to Nathan Cook, Elizabeth to Lewis Matthews, Mourning to Drury Matthews, and

Temperance to John Strother which four having been provided for in lifetime of the deceased were excepted from provisions of his will, will dated 19 October 1794, unmarried children John, Wiley, Susannah, Charity [page torn] Henry to be given Negroes, stock, and land in equal division. 959 ½ acres, 409 ½ acres on Mine and Little Saluda; deceased appointed John Strother and John Pope executors provided John Pope and his brother would carry on the farming and raise the children till they came of age, giving them schooling [following lines are torn, discolored and interwritten]. Plf charges that returns are deficient and imperfect. Charity Pope died 1796 under age and leaving no husband or children. Solomon Pope died 1798. Patience Robb formerly Patience Pope died in 1809 having a child who survived but a day or two and a husband James Robb who is entitled to a share of the estate. Henry Pope died intestate in 1810 leaving your oratrix his widow and one child the afsd Solomon L the ward of your orator who were then entitled the whole of his claim to the estate of his deceased father. Your orator married your oratrix in December 1813 and thereby became concerned with her in the admn of her deceased husband and is in law guardian of her son, Solomon L Pope. Asks that John and Ezekiel and Elizabeth may be compelled by decree of Court to account for and pay to orator and oratrix their proportion of estates of Solomon Pope Senr and of such of his children as have died leaving no children to represent them.

    Answer of John Pope. Deceased left 12 children: Mary then married to Burwell Cook, Elizabeth married to Lewis Mathews, Mourning married to Drury Mathews, and Temperance married to John Strother and the following unmarried John, Wiley, Susannah, Charity, Solomon, Henry, Patience, and Sampson. Lands, Negroes, and stock to be equally divided among unmarried children; believes part of estate was not devised and is liable to equal division among whole of children; has been sold under authority received from John Simkins Ordinary, for $179.76 ½. Deceased owned following Negroes: Tony, Sina, Doll, Hannah, Lydia, Winney, Lewis, Chloe, Peter. Wiley also admr of estate died 1800 or 1802. Exr managed estate, supported, raised, educated the children as required by will of testator, soon discovered that the plantation, labor of the Negroes, and income of estate would not meet the most economical and prudent management to support family in suitable manner. Dft and Wiley rebuilt grist mill and added a saw mill for which dft and his brother paid from their private funds about $550; some Negroes were infirm, others young and useless, without the aid of the mill the wish of the testator could not have been effected. Judgment in favor of estate against Thos Lamar. Before 1801 Susannah married Nathan Cook and was permitted the use of Lewis and Peter until the sale of the estate. About the same time Patience was permitted to use Chloe. In 1802 she married to James Robb at which time she had use of Sina and continued until Patience died in 1809 after which Chloe was hired out till the sale but Sina being small could not be hired for anything worth the trouble. In 1803 Wiley Pope's widow having married Ezekiel Nash, removed from the Hay's plantation. Henry Pope, late husband of complainant was permitted to occupy the plantation, negroes, stock and personal property for years 1803 and 1804. Henry managed the property badly, compelled by court to leave the plantation and property. Dozier & Johnston, Dfts sol. Sworn 25 October 1815.

    Answer of Ezekiel Nash. He had no knowledge of Solomon Pople's estate previous to August 1801. Sworn 16 May 1816. John Little guardian & Sarah Little vs John Pope exor, James Robb admr and E Nash admr. Appraisement 8 July 1812 by John (I) Dougles, John Salter, William Little; John Simkins, Ordinary. [In following lists any name is included only once; thereafter omitted.] Accounts paid 1795-1803 to Jno Cunningham, E Brenan, Dozier

& Bonnet, Francis Posey, P McDowall, Benj Lewis, Philip Eigner, A McFarlane, A McFarland, Danl Parkins, John Coudrey, Will Moore, Jona Nail, John Roberts, Tho Butler, Robt Burton, John Partlow, Hudson Bennett, Eugene Brenan. Estate accounts paid by Wiley Pope: William Roberts, George Mason, James Eidson, John Parnall, John Douglas, Garland Goode, George Roberts, John Corley, James Davis Senr, Jacob Adams, William Rice Clarke, Daniel Howell, Henry Smith, James Williams, Jane Leaford, Edward Caviach[?], Sarah Haddon, Ambrose Sanders, William Harris, Samuel Cotton, Nicholas Thomas, John Strother, James Davis Junr, William Coy, Isham Arledge, Francis Barnett, Thomas Deloach Senr, Elijah Warren, Dennis Gorgrit[Gorayoit?], Frederick Williams, Robert Seaford[Leaford?], William Deen, John Strother, Will Scott, W Demsey, Wright Nicholson, Daniel Wilson, James Mobley. Property sold 13 Decr 1813 of estate of Solomon Pope decd by John Pope exr: to John Pope 959 ½ acres with one acre taken by original claim of Isaac Hudson, to Sampson Pope Negroes Tony, Doll, Sary, Lyd & child Julius, boy Morress [Mossess?], boy Offy, Hannah & child Talitha, Sina the elder and Bob; Nathan Cook man Lewis, man Peter, girl Nance; John Pope girl Emly, girl Winney, girl Chloe; Nathan Cook man Peter; Nathan Cook girl Nance; Lewis Mathews Sina the younger; Drury Mathews, Ester; livestock to Ezekil Partain, Phillip Goode, Ezekl Partain, Phillip Goode, John Green. Property to Caleb Mauldin, Terry Davis, Nicholas Lowe, Daniel Potts, Samuel Davis, James Hudson, William Dozier, Chely Davis, Nathan Rowland, Nathan Cook. Isaac Gillion, Thomas Richardson. Receipts 1795-1798 Thos Harbirt, James Brooks, Ohn Bridges, John Duglass, Wm Haddon, Robert Allin, Abner Corley, Dennet Abney, Maryan Williams Davis, Wm Nicolson, Paul Abney, James Hays, Thos Dozier, Francis Posey, Nancy Duglass, Ephraim Ramsay, Benjn Wages, William Cain, Robert Newport, Saml Mays, Silvanus Walker, John Salter, Charles C Pinkney, Wm Little, Jno Stily, Edger Wills, Dozier & Bennet. Receipt Jan 3, 1803 from Ezekiel Nash; witness Mumford Perryman, James Bonham.

Decree, ordered that exor of Solomon Pope Sr to pay to James Rabb one moiety of estate which Patience his deceased wife would have been entitled to, and the remainder of what she was entitled to be distributed among her brothers and sisters & their representatives according to the act of 1791; Henry W DeSaussure. Decreed that in distributing the shares of such of the eight named chhildren of the testator as died under 21 years of age the same shall be divided among all their brothers & sisters & their representatives according to the act of 1791. Henry W DeSaussure.

#53   Meredith Wm Moon guardian of Andrew L Lark vs David Bates and others. Discovery & partition, 1819. Decree. Clause in will of Andw Lee deceased: "Item I will and bequeath to my beloved son Wilson Lee all the land lying on the North side of Saluda River below the road next to Manning and half the Bridge and two negroes named Jane & Frank, a horse of seven pounds and six cows & calves to be delivered to him when he arrives to the age of twenty one years to the above mentioned three sons and their heirs forever." In an after clause the testator says if any of my children should die without heir their estate to be equally divided among the rest of my children. Nancy Lee mother of the complainant was living at time of testator's death but died previous to Wilson Lee, who died before he arrived to age 21 and without issue Must have meant when he used the expression "die without an heir." The question is whether Andrew Lee Lark is entitled to the distributive share of Wilson Lee's estate which his mother would have been entitled to in the event of his having survived Wilson

Lee. Whether Wilson Lee meant the children living at the time of his own death, or such as should survive the legatee Wilson Lee. Court believes the intention was not to confine his bounty to his children only, but to expand it to his grandchildren, or why was the condition annexed that if any children should died without an heir, their share was to go to his other children. Order writ of partition issue to divide estate of Wilson Lee between parties entitled to a share thereof; dft pay costs of suit. W Thompson, 5 Feby 1819. Andrew Lee died December 1795, widow Nancy, children Susannah Lee. Hannah Patrick wife of Lewis Patrick, Nancy Lee afterwards Nancy Lark mother of your orator, Sarah Lee, Gersham Lee, John W Lee, and Wilson Lee. Susannah married Stephen Herndon, died [fold of paper obliterated date] leaving children. Gersham Lee and Wilson Lee died without lawful issue

#54   Rebecca Minter, William Minter, Richard Willborn and Pamelia his wife, Tandy M Key & Martha his wife vs McNess Minter, James Minter, Ebenezer Minter & John Minter, minors. [10 items] McNess Minter died leaving two tracts: 459 acres originally granted to William Holmes adj lands of Henry Key, 25 acres adj afsd tract, formerly owned by Abraham Martin, subject to be equally divided between your orators by virtue of an agreement whereby oratrix Elizabeth Minter agreed to take a child's portion, orator Richard Willborn & his wife received eighty acres by way of advancement which he is willing should be estimated by commissioners & deducted from his share of sd estate. Asks for writ of partition.
    Jeremiah Sigler, John Canfield, Stephen Thomas, Charles Nix, and Thomas Oglesby commissioned to divide equally if posible or to evaluate land. Stephen Tomkins JP.
    9 June 1819 appraisal, recommend land be sold, worth Nine Dollars per acre except Richard Wilborn & wife's advancement of 87 acres, worth $6.50 per acre.
    Answer of McNess Minter, James Minter, Ebenezer Minter & John Minter by guardian; willing to abide by decision of court.

#55   Catlett Conner, James Shackelford, Willis Mayson, Charles Mayson, executors of will of John C Mayson decd vs Admrs of J Bullock & others, Bill for specific performance. Filed 30 April 1818. [19 items] Testator about January 1808 purchased of John Bullock late of Edgefield, decd, land two hundred and[illeg] acres but titles not executed but a bond for $2000 entered, to be void upon execution and delivery by John Bullock to John C Mayson of good titles. Money paid by testator in his lifetime, accepted by [fold of paper obscured line of writing] leaving widow Rebecca Bullock since married to Col James Williams and children: John W Bullock, Duke M Bullock, George W Bullock, William P Bullock, James A Bullock, Joseph M Bullock, Eliza C Bullock, Lucinda A Bullock, Rebecca W Bullock, all minors under age of 21. Rebecca Bullock Williams with James Atwood Williams admr estate of John Bullock decd, James Atwood Williams has since died. John C Mayson died 2 December 1817 having made will & apptd orators exrs thereof. Willis Mayson one of orators has qualified. ltrs testamentary from Taliaferro Livingston ordinary of Abbeville District. John Bullock never executed titles to sd land. Asks that Rebecca Williams & husband and Bullock children by guardian execute titles.
    Answer of James and Rebecca Williams. James Gowdy executed title to land on 27 May 1797 to Matilda Smith who, after execution of title afsd, married William Williams and after the marriage sd Wm Williams and Matilda Smith sold sd land to John Bullock 13 January 1807. John Bullock afterwards sold sd land to John C Mayson and executed bond

for title to be executed agreeable to conditions, subject to terms of a further agreement 20 January 1808. John Bullock died leaving widow Rebecca Bullock and children. Rebecca Bullock and James A Williams admr. James died. John Bullock not bound to execute titles until the purchase money was paid. Rebecca is willing that titles be made in such manner as may be deemed by this Court. 1 Feb 1819. /s/ Rebekah Williams, /s/ James Williams.

Answer of John W Bullock, Duke M Bullock, George Washington Bullock, Wm P Bullock, James A Bullock, Joseph M Bullock, Elizabeth A Bullock, Lucinda Bullock, and Rebecca Bullock by their guardians ad litem James Williams and Rebeccca Williams. Their stepfather James Williams and Rebecca Williams their mother are able to attend to their interests and they submit to them, 5 June 1819. Bond of John Bullock unto John C Mayson in the village of Cambridge, Abbeville District, $2000, John Bullock to make title to 250 acres surveyed by Thomas Chiles D S adj Cambridge Commons, William Shaw, Ann Dunlap, William Williams, estate of Rev David Lilly decd; when John Mayson with Tolaver Bostick his security shall pay off their two notes of hand with interest and cost, above obligation to be void. /s/ John Bullock. Test Washington Bostick. John C Mayson was put in possession of the land eleven years ago, has since remained in peaceable and uninterrupted possession. There is now no suit for recovery of same land in name of William [nothing further]

#56   Samuel Marsh & wife vs Lavinia Blocker and others. Bill for sale. Samuel Marsh and Martha M Marsh complain that Michael Blocker seized two tracts of land, one adj Col Abner Blocker, of 250 acres; the other [page torn on fold of paper]. Oratrix widow of sd Michael Blocker is entitled to one third of sd land and her four minor children Lavinia Blocker, Julia Blocker, Adaline Blocker and James Blocker to the other two thirds. Being about to remove from this state, sale is necessasry. Ask for order to sell land. Filed 5 Feby 1819. Land to be sold. Grant to Samuel Marsh and his wife letters of guardianship of the children of Michael Blocker deceased.

#57   James Morgan, Francis Morgan and Lucinda Morgan by next friend Eli Morgan vs Martha Glover & others. Bill for partition. 11 January 1819. [12 items] William Glover died intestate leaving widow Martha Glover and children William, David, Matthew, Archibald Glover, Clarissa married to Samuel Mitchel, Elizabeth married to John Livingston, Mary married to Edward Holloway, Frances who married Thos Holloway, Martha who married Nathaniel Cowes[?], Amelia married to Museo Samuel, and Portia[?] married to your orator Eli Morgan and who died about 1818 leaving James, Francis and Lucinda Morgan their surviving children. Sd William Glover at time of his death possessed in his own right and in his wife of land on Dry Creek of Homes Creek and Savannah River adj lands of Henry Mealing, Robert Glover, J Lawless and John Martin, John Moore, land subject to division the heirs of William Glover decd. Asks for partition of land.

On motion of John S Jeter complainants solicitor, William Glover, David Glover, Saml Mitchell and Clarissa his wife, John Livingston and Elizabeth his wife, Thos Holloway and Francis his wife, Nathaniel Comes[?] defts reside without this state, given three months to answer or action will be taken. 8 June 1819 Commr Whit Brooks states it would be most advantageous to sell the land. Notice published in Chronicle & Gazette for three months; Editor, Kean & Co.

58   Jacob Lorry & Elizabeth Lorry vs Zacheus Woolley and others. Bill for partition. [15 items] Reason Woolley died 18— intestate leaving oratrix then Elizabeth Woolley and eight children: Zachariah, Sarah, Andrew, Vardry, Nancy, Reason, David, and that sd Sarah married William E Sawyers, that Reason Woolley before death had 302 acres on Lick Creek of Saluda River adj lands of Sheetz, Powel, Jacob Long, land at present undivided and unproductive to your orator now the husband of your oratrix as well to sd children. Asks partition be made and also appoint a guardian for sd minors, and summons to Zacheus Woolley, Sarah Sawyer and William E Sawyer, Andrew Woolley, Vardry Woolley, Nancy Woolley, Reason Woolley and David Woolley.

Commission to Nathan Norris, Jacob Long, Sion Mitchel, John Williams, and George Bowen, to go upon 302 acres on Lick Creek of Saluda River adj Hughes, Robert Atkins, Stents, Powel, land of late Reason Woolley, and partition between Jacob Long and wife Elizabeth Long, Zacheus Woolly, Sarah Sawyers and William Sawyers her husband, Andy Woolly, Vardy Woolly, Nancy Woolly, Reason Woolly and David Woolly, one third to Jacob Long and Elizabeth Long his wife, and assess value thereof, 1 Feby 1819; Butler. Land found to contain 304 acres in three tracts; recommend each tract be sold separately.

Answer of Zacheus Wooley, Andrew Wooley, Vardy Wooly, Nancy Wooly, Reason Wooley & David Wooley by guardian ad litem Zacheus Wooley; no objection to partition; 1 Feby 1819; /s/ Zacheus Woolley. Unsigned promissory note 29 January 1819 to pay Robert Marsh $12.50. Consent to partition 31 October 1818 /s/ Zacheus Woolley, /s/ Elizabeth (x) Woolley. Summons to Andrew Woolley, Vardry Woolley, Nancy Woolley, Reason Woolley and David Woolley, 3 Jany 1819 served by James Crane, special deputy; J Hatcher SED.

#59   Sarah Terry, guardian vs Joseph M Terry, Bill to authorize guardian to sell. Filed 8 June 1819. Sarah Terry, guardian of Joseph M Terry who is entitled to 293 acres on Beaver Dam Creek which was assigned to him by Commissioners apptd by Court as his share of real estate of his deceased father William Terry. It would be to advantage of sd minor to sell and terms have been stipulated with Elijah Bird but owing to minority of sd Joseph the contract cannot be completed. Asks permission to sell. Submits to judgment of Court; Whit Brooks. Authorize Sarah Terry to complete the sale to Elijah Bird [no date]. Concurrence of Col Jesse Blocker, Richard Christmas and John Bukhalter that sale is advantageous and that land be sold; 10 June 1819; Whit Brooks.

#60   Valentine Young & others vs Jonathan Young & others; Bill of Discovery & Relief. Abraham Young brother of your orator is a lunatic of unsound mind [page torn] In 1817 the Equity Court at Abbeville for Ninety Six District, further shews that Jacob Young the father of sd Abraham 10 June 1790 duly executed his will and amongst other things the following "Item I give unto my son Abraham Young the plantaiton whereon I now live of 270 acres to him and his heirs forever" and shortly afterwards departed this life leaving sd will. On 12 November 1802 Mary Cary (since deceased) the mother of sd Abraham and Jonathan Young brother of sd Abraham by deed of release procured sd Abraham and from them conveyed sd land to William Wrenn and Andrew Youngblood. Your orator charges that sd Abraham was incapable of making a conveyance of sd land. Sd Mary Cary and Jonathan Young by this unauthorized act have dispossessed Abraham of his property which his father had devised to him for support and maintenance. Your orator shows that William Wrenn and Andrew and Wm Wrenn, Andrew Youngblood, Asa Holloway, James L Jones and Douglas Holloway are now in possession [torn]. Asks sd conveyance be declared null and void .

Valentine Young vs William Wren, Andrew Youngblood and others. Answer of Andrew Youngblood. He purchased about 50 acres for $94, procured William Wren, Jonathan Young and Mrs Cary to join in the deed with Abraham. Abraham, although his mind somewhat below the ordinary, was competent. Abbeville District, 11 January 1819. /s/ Andrew Youngblood; Nathan Lipscomb JQ.

Answer of Asa Holloway, James L Jones & Douglas Holloway. Have possessed the land for about two years having purchased same from defts Wren and Youngblood. Know nothing of the sale to Wren and Youngblood. 25 Jany 1819; Abbeville District. /s/ Asa Holloway, /s/ James L Jones, /s/ Douglas Holloway; J M Cowdrey JP.

Answer of William Wren. Was advised to have the mother and eldest brother in the deed lest they might break the will. Well acquainted with Abram Young and all the family. Abram deformed in body, difficulty of speech, less informed than his brothers and sisters but evinced as much shrewdness in conversation as any of them; never saw any lunacy, knows the value of money. 30 Jany 1819; /s/ Wm (R) Wren; Robert Walker JP.

Deed to land granted to Jacob Young 16 February 1785 on Cuffeetown Creek. /s/ Mary (x) Cary; /s/ Jonathan (J) Young; /s/ Abraham (x) Young. Wit John Hamilton, James Anderson. Proved 27 March 1812 by James Anderson; Catlett Conner JP.

Will of Jacob (J) Young, 10 June 1790. Wit John Williams, Jonathan (x) Young, Charlotte (x) Young, Cresey (x) Burgess. Proved 3 sept 1792 by John Williams; R Tutt.

Deposition of Patrick Noble; was advised by George Bowie Esqr not to answer agst Jonathan Young, 7 June 1819; /s/ Patrick Noble. Confirmed by court.

A commission of Lunacy was granted. Verdict June 1817. Inquisition found him to be of unsound mind from birth without lucid intervals. Lunatic's father devised him 270 acres. 12 Nov 1802 Jonathan Young and Mary Cary mother of the lunatic and since dead procured sd Abram to join them and conveyed land to Wm Wrenn & Andrew Youngblood and they conveyed to Asa Holloway and others. Bill prays that they deliver up the deed to be cancelled & account for the rents and profits & put the said Abram into possession of the land. Noble Comp. Sol.

Dfts have used and occupied the land since 1803 to year 1820, making 17 years for which they are liable for rent. Dfts stand indebted to plf. Whit Brooks Comr

The finding of the jury overreached a sale & a deed executed 12 Nov 1802 by which Abram Young, his mother & brother had conveyed 270 acres , which land had been devised to Abram Young by his father for his support; his only means of support. Decree that sale of land in question be set aside, that the deeds of conveyance be delivered up to be cancelled, and that the defendants Wren, Youngblood account before the Commissioners for the rent & profits of the land from the time of the sale to the present. Henry W DeSaussure.

#61   William Quarles, John Quarles, & Richard Quarles et al vs Pleasant Thurmond, Bill for partition. Filed 9 June 1819. [10 items] Their father Richard Quarles died 1818 intestate leaving widow Sarah Quarles who has since married Pleasant Thurmond, also six children: John Quarles, William Quarles, Richard Quarles, Samuel Quarles, Hughy Quarles and Francy Quarles, the first two are of full age. Father Richard died possessed considerable estate both real and personal amongst which was two tracts of land lying on waters of Long Cane

Abbeville Dist, 691 acres adj land of Martin Tarants, J Morgan & heirs of [blank] Caldwell, and 340 undivided acres on Cuffeetown Creek in Edgefield. Orator prays Court to grant partition; if sd cannot be divided without injury to parties, to order sale.

Answer of Pleasant Thurmond and wife as guardians ad litem for Samuel Quarles, Hughy Quarles, and Francis Quarles, 9 June 1819. /s/ Pleasant Thurmond. From evidence of Commissioners Col John Key, Jesse Blocker, Wm Coursey the land cannot be divided, and that sale thereof would promote the interest of all parties; Whit. Brooks, 10 June 1819.

#62   Thomas Sheppard vs David Richardson, Charlotte Strother, and others. Bill for specific performance. Filed 26 May 1819. [9 items] Previous to death of George M Strother your orator purchased of him 183 acres in Lexington District adj lands of Bones, Pontnight & Swicard, for which sd George M bound himself to make titles as soon as last payment was made, your orator has paid all the purchase money to the admrs of sd Strother. Strother left widow Charlotte Strother and three minor children William, David, and George Strother. Sd Charlotte Strother & David Richardson, admrs estate of George M.are willing that title be made. Asks title to be made in name of sd minors and sd Charlotte Strother.

Answer of David Richardson & Charlotte Strother asks that plea be granted. /s/ David Richardson, /s/ Charlotte Strother; 28 May 1819; James Bell JP. Answers of William Strother, David, and George Strother by guardian ad litem Whitfield Brooks; submit to the judgment of the court.

Decree Whitfield Brooks, commr in Equity, to make titles to Thomas Sheppard, two thirds of purchase money for benefit of the sd minors and that Charlotte Strother make title to the sd Thomas of the remaining one third of sd tract. Henry Wm DeSaussure.

#63   Daniel McKie et al vs Abram & John Lundy. Bill for partition. Filed 3 Feby 1819. Orator Daniel McKie who married Nancy Lundy, Polly Lundy, and James Lundy show that their father Zach[h] Lundy died intestate leaving two minor children besides themselves under age 14, Abraham Lundy and John Lundy. Zachariah owned 275 acres on Gunnels Creek adj lands of Hezekiah Lundy and George Bussey. Minors by guardian ad litem Hezekiah Lunday submit to judgment of Court; /s/ Hezekiah Lunday. Bill for sale of land; much to advantage of parties that land be sold, 4 Feby 1819; Whit Brooks, Commr in Equity.

#64   Mark Huggins of Abbeville & wife Elizabeth vs Martin Witt. Filed 27 August 1818. [21 items] Elizabeth Huggins was daughter of Martin Hidle of Lexington Dist, decd, and only sister of John Hidle admr of Martin Hidle decd being his only children. Martin Hidle on 20 June 1817 possessed real and personal estate of $10,000. Oratrix separated from her father for about 20 years at distance of about one hundred miles, ignorant of her father, supposing him to be dead without making any provision for her. About 28 June 1817 Martin Witt, a perfect stranger, called on them and stated that he was acquainted with Martin Hidle, that he was living but had wasted his estate, that his property was of little value, that he was about to move to Alabama, proposed to orator and oratrix that he purchase of them their expectations of their father's land, and offered $45 for their share. Trusted to truth of what they had been told by Martin Witt but it was fraudulent fabrication on his part to deprive them of their rights at a price far below and inadequate to its real value. Stark, complts sol.

Answer of Martin Witt of Edgefield District. Denies charges against him. /s/ Martin Witt; Whit Brooks, CE ED.

Abbeville Dist, Deed, Elizabeth Hidle Huggins daughter of sd Martin Hidle to Martin Witt, her share of estate of Martin Hidle, $45, 27 June 1817. /s/ Mark (x) Huggins, /s/ Elizabeth (x) Huggins. Wit Joseph Williams, Nelley (x) Williams. Proved 27 June 1817 by Joseph Williams; Andrew Hamilton JQ.

June 1819. Bill seeks to set aside a deed of conveyance on grounds that Huggins is poor, illiterate, and weak, and also on grounds of extreme inadequacy of price. Mrs Huggins share turned out to be worth $2279, monstrous inequality. Add to this the extreme poverty and weakness of Huggins; Witt knew of the death of old Mr Hidle; he died on 15th June. Court cannot shut its eyes to injustice of the transaction. Deed is set aside; costs of suit to be paid by defendant. Henry Wm DeSaussure.

#65   John S Glascock vs GilbertLongstreet. Bill for Acct & Discovery. Filed 14 Sept 1819. Orator John S Glascock sheweth that Harden Blalock purchased of Gilbert Longstreet of Augusta merchandize on credit. To secure payment Harden Blalock mortgaged to Gilbert Longstreet five Negroes: Abraham, Abbe, Jack, Isaac, and Lett which are worth more than amount of purchase. Harden Blalock sent to Gilbert Longstreet in payment 52 rafts of lumber of 1500 ft each, which would amount to about $800 and also received a note amounting to $300 on [blank] of Abbeville District which your orator has been informed and believes has been collected by Gilbert Longstreet, that Gilbert Longstreet in 1818 came from Augusta and forcibly took possession of sd Negroes and carried them to Augusta and has kept them in his possession and sold two fellows for $2000 and one for $800 whereby Gilbert Longstreet has received considerable sum more than the original purchase money, that Harden Blalock on 2 April 1819 conveyed all his right in the Negroes to your orator and also assigned to your orator all his claim for damages against Gilbert Longstreet. Asks that Gilbert Longstreet may be compelled to come to fair settlement with orator and deliver to orator the Negroes in his possession and account with him for the value of those sold or account with him for the lumber received and the amount of the note above stated. Ellison, Complts sol

Mortgage of Negroes: Abraham fellow, Let wench, Jack, Abbe and Isaac fellows, for $3000 paid by John S Glascock, 2 April 1819. /s/ Harden Blalock. Wit F G Walton, J W Duncan.

#66   John Ramsay vs Eliza Goode admx. Bill for specific performance. Filed Feby 1819(sic). [6 items] In 1816 orator contracted with Mackerness Goode, now decd, for purchase of 358 acres. On 17 October 1816 Mackerness P Goode executed bond conditioned to be void if Mackerness Goode made sufficient title to sd tract on or before 1 January 1818. Mackerness Goode died 1818 intestate leaving wife Eliza Goode and one child, without having executed titles to sd land. Eliza Goode is admx and also has been appd gdn of minor child. Orator has paid all purchase money for sd land. Asks title to land. Mayson, Complts sol.

Answer of Eliza Goode. Is willing to abide by decree of Court. /s/ Eliza Goode; Charles C Mayson J P, 26 October 1818. Butler, dfts sol.

Order titles to tract be made and dft pay costs of suit out of the estate. W. Thompson.

#67   John G Riddle, Eleanor Riddle, James Riddle, Jesse Riddle, William Riddle, and

Louis Youngblood who married Mary Riddle, Daniel McRowe[M Rowe?] who married Sarah Riddle vs Martha & Thomas Riddle heirs of Wm Riddle, Bill for partition. Filed Feby 1819. Complts father died leaving eight children viz orators and Thomas Riddle who has since died leaving two minor children under age 14. Father died intestate, left land on Beaverdam Creek; asks partition of sd land. Glascock, sol.

Answer of Martha & Thomas Riddle by gdn Beverly Samuel; submit to decree of Court. Promissory note to Whitfield Brooks, 4 May 1819; signature torn off. Wit B Marsh. Settled in full. Batte Howard note $410; Whit Brooks. Receipt J Glascock, 7 May 1819. Whit Brooks report: impractable to divide the land, best to sell, 4 Feby 1819. Mistake made; there were but seven legatees. One third of proceeds of sale to be paid to Catherine Riddle.

#68   James Reese vs Edward B Holloway, Bill for relief [29 items] Filed 16 April 1818. In 1798 Reese possessed a negro woman Rody in Virginia. Being about to move to Georgia he left her in possession of Lewis Holloway in trust, to bring her with him. Lewis requested the loan of Rody; had her when he died. Rody has since had two children named Morris and Joicy. They are now in possession of Edward B Holloway admr of estate of Lewis Holloway; he purchased sd Negroes at sale of estate in full knowledge of claim of your orator. Asks Negroes be returned. Simkins & McDuffie, complts sols.

Answer of Edwd B Holloway. Had no knowledge of situation. Lewis Holloway did bring Rody many years past. Lewis Holloday who had quiet possession of Rody for 15 or 20 years. Jeter Defts sol. /s/ Edwd B Holloway, 1 June 1818.

A list of slaves and their ages: Jeaney 55; Eady sickly 25; Sarah 20, Violet 14, Harriet 5 children of Eady; Judah 4, Lucy & small child 23, Silla 9. Viney, 7, Nancy 4, Barbra 13, Joe 8, Viney 19, Jim 5, Rhoda 4.

Subpoenas to Saml Williams, Wm Pursell, John Moore, Thos Webster, Rachel Holloway, 1 June 1818. Deposition of Justice Barksdale Gardner; In January Thomas O Holloway offered to sell him a Negro wench Viney and her two children James and Rhody for $800 given good title; had information they were property of James Reese at the death of Mrs Rachel Holloway the mother of sd Thomas Holloway; Gardner declined sale. Depositions of John Sullivan 20 May 1822, John Miller, Thos McKie, Wiley Glover. Deposition of James Reese 11 October 1817; Eldred Simkins QU.

Lewis Holloway was father of deft and died October 1814. Witnesses declared they had heard Lewis Holloway state that Rhody was property of Reese. Lewis Holloway had several other slaves during the lifetime of his wife & at her death they were to go to her daughter who was Reese's wife but Rhody could be taken by Reese when he pleased. Dft immediately to deliver Rhody, Joicy and Morris to complainant. Commissioner to report what may be due to complainant for hire & labor from the time of his making a demand for her. Henry Wm De Saussure.

#69   Lark Abney admr of will annexed of John Abney vs Lemuel Munson, Bill for specific performance. [9 items]   Lemuel Munson on 1 December 1810 bound himself to make titles to sd John Abney of 150 acres granted to Daniel McKie on Beaver Dam Creek providing if sd Munson paid £33.6.5 within 12 mos to be in full force; Munson did not pay sd sum in specified time nor has he yet paid it.   Answer of Lemuel (x) Munson 8 June 1819.

Subpoena to Saml T Shanklin, Harriet Shanklin, Maryelda Tillman, Benjn Tillman,

GENEALOGICAL ABSTRACT OF EDGEFIELD EQUITY COURT RECORDS

William Moore alias William Coleman, 13 January 1819; Butler.

Subpoena to Benjamin Tillman & wife Mary Elder, Elizabeth Moore and William Moore otherwise called William Gallman by Benjamin Gallman his guardian. Butler, atty.

Wm Butler & Bld Butler vs Saml Shanklin & others, 23 Jany 1819, served by Leontine Butler; Wm Jerguson JP.

Henry Wm DeSaussure orders Lemuel Munson execute titles for sd land to complt.

#70 William Ponds who married Mary Rambo, Swan J Brown who married Martha Rambo, James Rambo and Matilda Rambo, Albert Rambo by their guardian Fielding Reynolds vs Augustus Rambo, Bill for Partition. Filed 4 Feby 1819. [8 items].   Their father died possessed of 270 acres on road from Edgefield Court House to Augusta adj lands of John Day and James Longstreet. Asks land be partitioned. Glascock sols.

Answer of Augustus Rambo by Fielding Reynolds guardian, in consequence of tender age they submit to decree of Court, 4 Feby 1819. /s/ Fielding Rennolds.

Jos Rambo to his wife Susannah Chany Rambo and my children Mary Moore, Martha Scantling, Reuben, James, Matilda Elizabeth and Albert Jefferson, official copy. Five Negroes girl Dilsey, girl Silver, girl Lucy, girl Fanney, boy Toney and girls' increase, live-stock and furniture, 4 February 1800. Witness C Martin Jr, Fielden Renolds. /s/ Jos Rambo. Proved 5 Feb 1805 by Fielding Renolds; John Blocker JP.

Wm & Beverly Samuel & Fielding Runnels report that the land, a small tract of pine land, cannot be divided; interests of parties promoted by sale; Whit Brooks 4 Feby 1819.

Film No.Jr.4070

#71 Isaac Parker trustee of Elizabeth Parker and Elizabeth Parker vs Geo Parker. Sale of trust estate. [items]. Filed 2 Feby 1819. Benjamin Mazyck by will bequeathed £600 for Elizabeth & her children. [paper torn on fold] 700 acres in Edgefield on which Elizabeth and her husband George Parker lately resided, orator has agreed with James Longstreet to sell him the land; proceeds decreed to her. Simkins & McDuffie.

Answer of George Parker. He concurs in propriety of sale. /s/ George Parker.

Whit Brooks, 4 Feby 1819, Benjamin Hightower Senr, John Moore and Stephen Garrett concur that the sale is advantageous. Sale ordered, Feby 5, 1819; /s/ W Thompson.

Ex parte George Parker, 28 October 1816 sold land which had been settled in trust for benefit of himself and family and purchased another tract for $5000, considerable amount still remained unpaid, to secure payment of which George Parker mortgaged to Wm Harden. Further sale to Jas Longstreet; Longstreet has purchased the mortgage given by George Parker to Wm Harden on which a balance of $500 is unpaid; estate injured by failure to complete the contract; mortgage stands as an incumbrance; Isaac Parker should allow the discount insisted on by Longstreet; Whit Brooks. June 1819.

#72 Morris P Holloway & wife Rebecca Moore Holloway widow of Anderson Moore decd vs William Anderson Moore et al, Bill for Partition. Filed 8 June 1819. [7 items] Anderson Moore died 1815 intestate leaving widow and children William Moore, Right N Moore, Mary Ann Moore. Anderson Moore possessed 600 acres on Mountain Creek adj lands of Jordan Holloway, John Mitchel, Spencer Smith. Asks partition or sale. Glascock, sol.

Answer of John Terry Sr guardian of William Anderson & Jordan Holloway, guardian ad litem of Right N Moore & Mary Ann Moore; submit to decree of Court; /s/ John Terry Sr, Jordan Holloway. 8 June 1819; Whit Brooks CEED. Jas Blocker. Jordan Holloway & Dabney Palmer report sd land is poor and badly watered; impractical to divide; land to be sold. /s/ Whitefield Brooks, 9 June 1819.

#73   Phillip Herrin et al vs Fedrick Holmes & Patience his wife. Bill for partition. [4 items] Phillip Herrin who married Mary Swearingham, Josiah Swearingham, Van Edward Swearingham, James Stalnaker married Patsey Swearingham. Their father Rice Swearingham died some years since intestate leaving his children and a widow who has since married Frederick Holmes, leaving 300 acres on Horse Creek adj lands of John Landrum, Steven Williams as yet undivided. Asks writ of partition. Glascock, solr
        Answer of Fedrick Holmes and wife Patience submit to decree of Court. /s/ Frederick Holmes. /s/ Patience (x) Holmes, 4 Feby 1819; Whit Brooks CEED

#74   Benjamin Frazier exr and Rebekah his wife, Eleanor Rearden & Emeline Rearden; Bill for partition. [11 items] William Rearden died intestate in August 1812 leaving widow Rebekah Frazier and two children Eleanor and Emeline. Sd Wm Rearden with his brother Timothy Rearden decd 1 January 1807 joinintly purchased of Armstead Hall 223 ½ acres on Turkey Creek by resurvey 447 acres which land remains undivided. Widow Rebekah Frazier purchased of Jordan Holloway sd Timothy Reardon's undivided moiety of sd tract. Asks Court to partition two thirds of one half of sd land. Jeter, solr
        Commission to Wilson Kemp, Frederick White, John Arledge Sr, John Jenkins, and John Arledge Junr to lay off two thirds of one half of land or to recommend sale. Comissioners recommend that same be sold, 27 May 1819. /s/ Wilson Kemp, /s/ John (x) Arledge, /s/ Fred White. Answer of Eleanor and Emeline Rearden by guardian ad litem Whitfield Brooks, submit to decree of Court. Benj Frazier and wife vs Eleanor and Emeline Rearden

#75   Thomas N Frazier vs John Stedham et al. [5 items] Answer of John Frazier exr and John Stedham on behalf of himself and wife and guardian ad litem for John M Frazier and Sarah Adaline Frazier. He submits to decree of Court. 4 June 1819. /s/ John Frazier, /s/ John (x) Stedham. Commissioners recommend land be sold.

#76 is missing.

#77   Nancy Clark, William Dean and wife Catherine formerly Catherine Clarke vs Leonard Clarke and others. Bill for partition. Filed 10 May 1819. [8 items] Aaron Clarke husband of oratrix Nancy and father of Catherine died intestate in January 1815 possessed of land on Red Bank Creek adj William Adams, Richard Dozier. David Richardson. To be divided between sd Nancy Clark the widow of Aaron Clarke decd, William Dean in right of his wife Catherine formerly Catherine Clarke, Thomas Clarke, Leonard Clarke and James Clarke the only surviving chldren and legal representatives of sd Aaron Clark. Asks that Thomas Clarke, Leonard Clarke and Jame Clarke be subpoenaed to show why prayer of oratrix should be granted. Jeter, solr
        Answer of Thos Clarke, Leonard Clarke, and James Clarke by guardian ad Litem James Scott, submit to decree of Court. 8 June 1819. Report of commissioners Thomas Scott,

GENEALOGICAL ABSTRACT OF EDGEFIELD EQUITY COURT RECORDS

Sampson Butler, Jas M Butler, James A Harris and Richard Bullock: to the interest of the parties that the land be sold. 9 June 1819.

#78   Charles O'Neal and wife Charlotte, Arthur Dillard and wife Polly, Nathaniel Townsend and wife Elizabeth, Jacob P Abney, Sarah J M Abney, and Ann Abney which two last appear by guardians Susannah Spearman & Edward Spearman, also Joseph Rearden & wife Nancy vs Lark Abney, Henry M Abney, Jonathan Abney and Ira Abney. Bill for partition. [23 items] John Abney died some years past leaving a will which directs the lands hereinafter described to be equally divided between your orators and Lark Abney, Henry M Abney, Jonathan Abney and Ira Abney. Sd land consisted of 1700 or 2000 acres adj Saluda River, Zach S Brooks, John Julow[?], Azariah Abney, Sarah Carson, Crawford Perry, Paul Abney, Irbin Nicholson; also 200 acres on Cuffeetown Creek. To the interest of all parties to have sd lands divided or sold. Simkins & McDuffie comps sols.
        Answer of Lark Abney, Henry M Abney, Jonathan Abney, and Ira Abney by guardian Lark Abney submit to judgment of the Court. /s/ Lark Abney, 8 June 1819.
        Zachariah S Brooks, Sampson Pope the elder, John Abney junr, Reuben Coleman & William Coleman Esqrs: Commissioners to evaluate and divide land, if cannot be fairly divided make return thereof. Simkins & McDuffie, plfs sols.
        Cannot divide without manifest injury to parties, 3 August 1819; /s/ Z^th Brooks, Sampson Pope, John Abney, Reuben Coleman, William Coleman. Land to be sold 26 July 1819. John G Peterson JP.
        Commissioner has $330 the share of Lark Abney decd of the proceeds of land sold, that Sampson Pope as guardian of Ira Abney has obtained decree against the curators of Lark Abney for a large amount which remains unsatisfied, order commissioners pay over sd money taking a receipt for same; Henry W Desaussure, 20 June 1828. Plat of four tracts of land [too faded to read on microfilm]. Suits: Hugh Johnson vs John Johnson; John Deen vs John Parker, John Wall vs Wm Wall, Joseph Hatton vs H Blalock.
        Charles O'Harrah & wife vs Lark Abney, recommends that land in question be sold 1 Monday in May next; 10 Feby 1820; Whit Brooks.
        Dr Charles O'Neall & wife & others vs Lark Abney. It appear to court that sale of land called Michler tract on Cuffee Town Creek adj lands of Frederic Slappy was not ordered, sd tract being subject of litigation with Joseph Stallworth; suit has been decided in favor of heirs of Abney; orders sd land sold 1st Monday in May next.

#79   James O'Hara & wife Cynthia vs Jane Cobb & others. Partition. Filed 23 May 1816. [67 items] Cynthia is a daughter of James Cobb planter who died 1801 intestate leaving widow Jane Cobb and five children besides complainant: James, Thomas, Sophrony since deceased, John S Cobb and Elizabeth now minors above age 14. Intestate possessed Negroes, horses, cattle, chattels, debts, &money owed him. Jane Cobb with John Blocker Sr admrs, securities Daniel Bird and Joseph Walence. Sale $9183.92 3/4. Sept 11John Blocker returned inventory of cash & debts $1061.01 3/4. Intestate resided on Horns Creek; but his Mother Barbara Cobb claimed a proportion and occupied during her life for 3 or 4 years after his death. Thomas Cobb Sr, brother of intestate, after latter's death held possession of land 3 or 4 years before Jane Cobb obtained full possession thereof during which time a lawsuit was depending which was not ended till it was ascertained that Thomas Cobb Sr had no right to any part of sd land; it belonged to intestate James Cobb and hath since vested in his heirs. During the time Thomas Cobb Sr was in possession these complts are ignorant of what use and by whom was made of cultivated parts of land or what waste had been done on other parts or what steps have been made by adminx and admr to secure rents, profits, or compensation. After suit with Thos Cobb Sr ended admr or admx had full possession. Same has occupied from 1808 to 1814 both inclusive & rents thereof used without regard to share of complts. Sophrony a daughters of sd intestate died. Demand their proportional share of her part. James Cobb and Thomas Cobb sons of intestate & half brothers to this complt Cynthia. Sd James and Thomas Cobb received greatest part of their shares as distributees of their father's personal property yet these complts believe the whole has not yet been paid to them. John Blocker admr of sd estate died about 1814; his will named his widow Juliana and her sons John and James extx and extr thereof. James Cobb grandfather of Cynthia Cobb died intestate possessed of considerable estate. Barbara Cobb his widow and his sons James and Thomas Cobb admrd; amount of his estate was $6128.52 1/2. Complts are entitled to distributive share thereof in right of her father; are informed that such share has been received by sd Jude Cobb or the sd John Blocker. Complt James Ohara states that 10 July 1814 he married Cynthia whereby he claims in right of his wife to be entitled to her share. Asks that subpoenas issue to Jane Cobb, Juliana Blocker, James Blocker, John Blocker, James Cobb, Thnomas Cobb, John S Cobb, and Eliza Cobb, and that writ of partition be issued. Goodwin, solr.

Report of admr John Blocker, yearly sales and distribution. Sum advanced to Jane Cobb, a proportion of which was appropriated to support of Mrs Oharra then a minor living with her mother; such proportion should be credited in account of dft. Whitfield Books, 28 May 1879. Situation of Mrs. Jane Cobb from death of her husband to the marriage of Mrs Oharra in 1814 to raise and educate her children, Evidence produced was of uncertain nature. The witnesses representation of situation of Mrs Cobb as being always a little embarrassed, able during some years to make a support and at others unable.

Separate answer of Jane Cobb. Husband James Cobb died 29 April 1801 leaving children by present wife and James Cobb and Thomas Cobb by a former marriage. Being ignorant of keeping accounts, that part of management was done by John Blocker and after his death by James and John Blocker his executors. Jane purchased from James and Thomas Cobb their right to their distributive shares. She has cultivated only the land meted off for her; at estate sale she purchased to the full amount of her distributive share; did not purchase within $500 of her distributive share of property sale. James, her deceased husban's father died intestate; his widow Barbara Cobb died intestate after her husband. Between their deaths dft's husband died. Sale of James Cobb's property took place after death of younger James Cobb. Family maintenance devolved upon Jane. Three of her only 4 working Negroes died. She was obliged to draw money from co-admr money at different times for maintenance, education, & clothing of her children. Sworn 26 May 1819 /s/ Janey Cobbs; Whit Brooks.

Answer of James Blocker & John Blocker. Defence of their father's and their actions in administrating estate of the intestate James Cobbs. 19 May 1817. Mrs Juliana Blocker swears facts are true, 24 May 1817; /s/ Juliany Blocker. [In the following accounts, a name is listed only once] 1803 list of cash paid to Thos Tillman, John Gray Senr, Henry Brigs, Robt Graduel[?], Doct Wm Braziel, Thomas Garrett, Butler Williams, John Hugh, Mathew Mays, John Ryan, Mary Hodges, John Hall, William Hill, William Jeter. E Whatley to James Cobbs decd. Paid Christopher Shaw. Cash rec'd: Ransom Hamilton, John Lucas, James West,

Zachariah James, Stephen Mays, Charles Mitchel, Hinchey Mitchel, Edwd Mitchel, James Runols, David Tillman, Daniel Parker, Charles Martin Senr, Charles Hammond, Seth Howard, Thomas P Martin, Joseph Griffin, Daniel Macus, Samuel Marsh, David Donalson, William Walls, Thomas Traylor, Thomas Cobbs, Charles Randolph, John Rudisill, William Powel, Little Berry Adams, Robert Marsh, Isome Franklin, Moses Spear, Richard Boosh, Onemus Fudge, Federick Tillman. Examined 3 July 1804 and find vouchers for all. Jno Simkins OED. Cash paid 1804 cash paid: V P Williams, Benjn Adams, Fielding Runnels, William Scales, William Wash, Isaac Randolph, Benjn Lindsey, Ab G Dozier, Moses Spears, William Jeter, John Murrey, Nicholas Cooper, William F Tayloe. Received: Aaron Watson, David Clark, Ezekiel Robuck, John Runnols, Joseph C Ried, Joseph Collier, Sampson Butler. Received 1801: Abraham Lucas, John Rudsill, Thomas Wallpool, Garlan Snead. Cash paid 1805: William Grissom, Michael Blocker, John Simkins, Abraham Dozier. 1805 received from John C Allen, Charles Martin Jr.

Decree June 1819: Ordered that the Commissioner's report be confirmed and that the costs of suit be paid by administrator out of the assets in his hands. Henry W DeSaussure.

#80   Thos Burnett and others vs Robt Burnett & Anthony Burnett, Partition. [11 items] [torn] Hasting and wife Elizabeth, Jeremiah Bur[torn], Thomas Burnett, Catharine Burnett, William Burnett, & Hezekiah Burnett that Jeremiah Burnett [page torn along fold of paper] deed of gift to orator & Robert Burnett & Anthony Burnett his children: Negroes: Sarah, Abram, Poll, Hall, Sam, Charles; also 300 acres which he bought of his brother Sanders Burnett, 200 acres being part of 300 acres bought of John Adams, 100 acres which he bought of George Slater, 100 acres which he bought of Henry Strum and property [torn along fold in paper] till his death. Jeremiah Burnett died 29 December 1814 intestate whereby sd property became vested in your orators & oratrix. Partition desired. Jeremiah Burnett also left considerable personal estate. His widow Elizabeth Burnett & Lark Abney administered estate & also 250 acres, 150 of which adjoins the land mentioned in sd deed, other hundred acres lie on Mountain Creek. Elizabeth Burnett claims her dower of sd land included in the deed as well as her distributive share of the land & personal property not deeded therein.

Answer of Robert & Anthony to bill of complaint of Benjamin Hasting & Elizabeth his wife, Jeremiah Burnett, Thomas Burnett, Catharine Burnett, William Burnett & Hezekiah Burnett say that complainants are entitled to respective share of lands and negroes mentioned, that Jeremiah Burnett died possessed of other lands besides those contained in the sd deed, that they are willing that partition be made of property in sd deed and property not included therein and negroes mentioned in sd deed. Glascock, dft sol. Benjamin Hasting swears that matters contained above are true, 6 Feby 1818; /s/ Benjamin Hasting; Whit Brooks CEED.

Robt Burnett & Anthony Burnett vs Eliz Burnett & others, filed 6 Feby 1818. Joint answer of Anthony Burnett and Robert Burnett by their guardians Jeremiah Burnett & Benjamin Hastings. These dfts are minors & submit to decree of court. /s/ Benjamin Burnett guardian of Robert. /s/ Jeremiah Burnett guardian of Anthony. Sworn 1 June 1818; /s/ Benjamin Hasting, /s/ Jeremiah Burnett. Whit Brooks CEED

Thos Burnett & others vs Robert Burnett & Anthony Burnett & others. The named Negroes are unproductive; need a speedy division of them. Negroes were deeded to complts and Jeremiah's children Robert Burnett and Anthony Burnett. [List of Negroes here includes Kate] Ask writ of partition be directed to Wiley Kemp & George Nichols on part of complts and Robert Walker and Davis Williams on part of dfts & Philip Dillard nominated by court by consent of parties to divide Negroes.

Copy of Deed of Gift, 14 January 1815, Jeremiah Burnett for love to his children: Elizabeth Hasting, Jeremiah, Thomas, Isaac, Katharine, William, Hezekiah, Robert & Anthony. /s/ Jeremiah Burnett. Witness Samuel (U) Williams. /s/ Peggy (x) Walker.

#81   Polly Buffington & Matilda, Hester, James, Joseph, Henry and Polly Buffington the younger by next friend & guardian Polly Buffington the elder vs Abner Clark & Elijah Lyon. Bill for Discovery & Relief. [items] Henry Clarke father of Polly Buffington and grandfather of Matilda, Hester, James, Joseph, Henry and Polly Buffington the younger died testate leaving all real and personal estate to his wife Molly alias Mary and at her death to be equally divided between his children. Widow Molly survived her husband for considerable time. Abner Clark her son, brother of your oratrix administered her estate. Before Molly's death she gave oratrix Negro woman Fan and unborn child; she gave Abner a girl Lise; to Tilly Buffington boy Ephraim, to Patcy Clarke woman Fan & her children all rightful property of oratrix. Yet Abner Clarke and Elijah Lyon knowing gift was made confederated with husband of oratrix, giving him some trifling gift, to defraud Polly of Fan and increase. Abner Clarke sold Fan and her children Ben, Cate and [blank] to Elijah Lyon; he also bought negro fellow George, son of Fan and property of your oratrix. All intended to be for Molly Clarke are in possession of Abner who holds a Negro boy Sammy; Patcy Clark holds fellow Ephraim. Polly Buffington states she has not received her distributive share of property left by her father Henry Clarke to equal proportion to which she was entitled. Abner Clarke took sd property and has refused to account with her. Asks for her share of property. Bacon, complts solr.

Answer of Abner Clarke and Elijah Lyon. After Henry Clarke died, widow Mary remained in possession of his estate but of what property sd estate consisted they canot state. Abner admrd estate of his mother Mary Clar October 1812. Mary's estate including Negroes amounted to $1954.10 3/4. Negro Fan was given by Mary to her daughter Polly Buffington, other gifts were made to Mary; he further states that Polly Buffington gave back Negro Fanny to her Mother to prevent her husband's children by his first wife from obtaining any share of his or her increase, further states that Polly Buffington and her husband agreed that Abner as admr of his mothers' estate should sell Fanny and her issue as the estate of Molly Clarke on the condition that the purchaser should keep & maintain her young child and at 12 months deliver it to Polly Buffington or Richard Buffington her husband, that afsd agreement was made on the very day on which Fanny & her children were sold. In conformity with afsd agreement the negro was tendered to Polly Buffington which she refused to receive; Abner knows nothing about the administration of Henry Clarke's estate.   Sales of Mary Clarke's state were made in 1813. Abner purchased Negro George for $178; Elijah Lyon purchased Fan for $301, and son for $113; George is about six years old. At present, value of Negroes is now about $300. He holds boy Sam, Patsey Clark boy Stephen[?] under gift of Mary Clarke but begs leave to state that Matilda Buffington daughter of Polly holds under same gift the Negro girl Lise. Annual value of Negroes, most of them being useless, cannot be considered. Abner states that he has made regular returns of his doings except one year when his health would not permit him to do so, that Richard Buffington was indebted to the estate at his death $870.11 ½ which is much more than the distributive share of Polly Buffington which debt appears by two promissory notes and an account herewith filed.   He believes that mother was at time of the gift not in sound mind and memory. Elijah Lyon saith he purchased Negroes Fan & Ben at sale of Mary Clarke's estate fairly and had no doubt as to the validity of the sale. /s/ Abner (x) Clark; /s/ Elijah Lyon. Sworn 10 August 1816; Whit Brooks, CEED.

Polly Buffington vs Abner Clark. Evidence taken 21 January 1820. William Nelson swears that Elijah Lyon got possession of wench Fanny about 5 or 6 years ago. She had at that time two children, one very young, two other children have been born since that time. Maintenance of the children has since that date been more than the services of the wench are worth. It is his opinion that no breeding wench is worth more than her supposrt.

John Morris swears he concurs.

30 January 1820. Champion Welborn swears he saw the girl five or six years ago. She is a likely wench. She was a taskable hand when he knew her & has been ever since. That for 5 or 6 years she has been worth $25 per annum.

John Timmerman swears he saw wench Fanny the day Lyon bought her; she for 6 years she has been worth $25 annually.

Jacob Wideman swears he has known wench 15 years; she is worth $25 per year.

James Cox swears he has known Fanny for many years; worth $25 per year.

Reports on George. [name obliterated] boy worth $15 per annum. Wm Welborn same. Wideman same. Cox thinks boy worth nothing. Henry Stone swears boy George has been an expence to Clark. George was born in 1808. Hire of George for the year 1819 $7.50. Abner Clark liable for $7.50; Whit Brooks CEED. February 2, 1820.

Account of sales, estate of Mary Clarke 9 January 1813. Sales to John Findley, Wm Hammond, Robert Perrin, James Cox, Richd Buffington, Wm Burt, Abner Clark, Abraham Lassitter, Susannah Clark, Joshua Carr, Henry Cosper, Mathew Barrett, James Tutt, Alex Moseley, Hugh Moseley, H A Nixon, Doctor Ellison, Peter Caulk, Harman Cosper, James Atcheson, John Norton, Peggy Mark, Daniel Selpht, Robert Yeldale, Wm Nelson, Joseph Norris, William Price, Benjn Perry, Wm Shannon, George Sullivan, Lewis Hammond, John Littleton, James Carson, Frederick Knop, James Cunell Esqr.

Decree. Council for complt introduced George H Cooper, minister of the gospel, a man of unblemished and fair reputation who swears he saw Mrs. Clarke take the hand of the Negro Fanny and put it into the hand of the Complt Polly Buffington and said I give you this Negro and her increase to you and the heirs of your body forever. Mrs. Cooper wife of George H Cooper testified to same facts verbatim; they together with Larkin Cason were called on to witness sd gift. Cason swears that he was present and saw Mrs. Clarke give to the Complt the Negro Fanny and that the gift was absolute to her. Evidence is decidedly in favor of the Complt. The property was never considered as Buffington's. Mrs Clarke has been repeatedly heard to say that she has not given these Negroes to Polly and her children; she must have been out of her senses as she could not rest in her grave if she thought Buffington or his children were to have any share in the Negroes. Besides if Buffington's right has been considered good, why would he have sacrificed so valuable a property for so inconsiderable a consideration as a small Negro child. Moreover wherefore sell this property as property of Mrs Clarke's estate. It was evident she had no right to it, having previously given it either to the Complt absolutely or to her and the heirs of her body. Ordered sale be set aside and the Negroes be restored to the Complt and that the defdt do account before the commissioner for their hire. It is also decreed that the Dft pay costs of this suit. W. Thompson.

File Number 82 is missing.

No. 83. Jeremiah Burnett et al vs Elizabeth Burnett & others. Bill for partition. [11 items]
Henderson Barnes v Catharine Barnes and others. Bill for sale of land. Filed 1 Feby 1819. Orator Henderson Barnes complains that Benedict Barnes died possessed of 150 acres on Dry Creek or Buckhalters Creek adj lands of C Breithaupt, James Bilbo, and John Fox, and leaving Henderson Barnes, Catharine Barnes, Benedict Barnes, and Susanna Barnes his children heirs at law entitled to his estate who are also minors under the age of twenty one. Orator desires land be sold & purchase money put out at interest until children come of age. During a long minority the land would either be idle or be cultivated in a wasteful manner by those who may rent it and the land may become worn out and worth but little.

Answer of Catharine Barnes, Benedict Barnes, & Susanna Barnes by their guardian Jonas Lanham. It would be advantageous to sell the land.

Jeremiah Burnett, Thomas Burnett, Isaac Burnett, Benjamin Hastings and wife Elizabeth, Gazaway Rogers & wife Catherine, Anthony Barnett who sues by his guardian Jeremiah Burnett, Luvanna Burnett who sues by her guardian [blank] vs Elizabeth Burnett & others. Jeremiah Burnett Senr died intestate leaving land [blank] to be distributed amongst your orators & Martin Burnett, Marian Burnett & Elizabeth M Burnett all children of decd, after assigning to Elizabeth Burnett widow of decd her one third part thereof. It is to the interest of the parties that sd lands be sold. Filed 8 Jan 1819.

Henderson Barnes & Catharine Barnes & others. Commissioners to determine whether sale is to benefit of minor children or not. Answer: land cannot be divided equitably; recommend sale; J Terry. Money to be put out at interest, 4 Feby 1819; Whit Brooks CEED.

Jeremiah Burnett & others vs Eliz Burnett & others. To benefit of children that land be sold. Writ of partition issues to commissioners James Monday, Hezekiah Nobles, James Harrison, Edward Balser & Richard Lewis.

#84 Millington Blalock & others against Thomas Tally and wife & others. Bill for partition or sale, [13 items] Filed 11 September 1818. On behalf of myself as guardian for the minor children of Abel Hill decd I accept service of writ, Marg (x) Hill. As deft I appear in behalf of my self & wife; D M Loveless. As guardian of my daugher Harriett Hill I accept writ; Mary (x) Hill. In behalf of myself & Mahulda my wife I consent to writ; James Tomkins. Samuel Hill died September 1815 leaving widow Mary Hill and nine children: Elizabeth married to Thomas Tally, Susan married John Kilcrease, Mahulda lately married James Tomkins, [blank] who married William Jennings who is left a widow without children. Sarah who married Millington Blalock, Mary who married David Lovelace, Lavica to Robert Jennings, Nancy married Cornelius Cox, Harriet Hill, and Abel Hill who has since died leaving a widow Margaret Hill and the following children, Elizabeth, Sally, Priscilla, Narcissa, Sarah, Samuel, John, William, and Abel who are entitled to sd Abel's part. Land: 200 acres on Gunnels Creek of Stephens Creek adj lands of Sander C Herring, Thomas Stephenson, Levi Harden. Also 493 ½ acres on Stephens Creek adj lands of Elezer Odonal, John Kilcrease, which was granted to Samuel Hill 4 March 18 [blank]. Also 150 acres conveyed by Minor Kilcrease to sd Samuel Hill and surveyed for William Jeter on 18 February 1793 situate on branches of Beaver Dam and Gunnels Creek adj lands of John Thurmond, Roger Smith, sd Saml Hill, Henry Key. Eighteen acres adj lands of [blank]

Crawford. James Thomas, Widow Thomas, surveyed 10 Nov 1785 on waters of Savannah River. Nine acres on Stephens Creek adj Sandifer's land, Widow Hill, surveyed for sd Saml Hill 11 Novr 1785. Mary Hill widow of Samuel Hill is entitled to one third part. The eight children now living with sd widow, and children of Abel Hill decd are entitled to remaining two thirds in equal shares. Asks writ of partition or sale. Simkins & McDuffie.

Commissioners John Glanton, John Lyon, William Holmes, Thomas Kilcrease and William Hardy appointed. To return recommendation June Court 1819.

Commissioners evaluated tracts, recommend sale, 9 Jund 1819; /s/ John Glanton, /s/ John Lyon, /s/ William Homes, /s/ Thos (T) Kilcrease, /s/ Wm Hardy; Shurley Whatley J P.

#85   James Beams & others vs Harriet W Beams. Bill to authorize trustees. [7 items] Samuel Walker and [blank] trustees for Rebecca Beams & her issue, & also your orator James Beams & your oratrix, Rebecca Beams. Some years past the sd James Beams owing to infirmities made a deed of trust by which [line of writing lost in torn fold of paper] called the Valley of Hope near Edgefield Court House containing one[?] hundred acres in trust for Rebecca Beams and her issue by James Beams; Court lately substituted Hinchell Mitchell as a trustee in place of Samuel Marsh. James Beams about to remove to Alabama Territory where the brother and trustee of your oratrix Rebecca Beams has already gone. Beams has agreed with Charles Goodwin Esq to convey the land to Charles Goodwin. Trustees approve. Inasmuch as Samuel Walker resides at great distance from this place, orators & oratrix pray to authorize Hinchell Mitchell in name & behalf of himself and Samuel Walker Jr to make title for sd land to Charles Goodwin Esq when he shall have paid Twelve hundred Dollars, sum to be held by trustees for Rebecca Beams & issue by James Beams: Harriet W Beams, Ann T Beams, Emala M Beams. Simkins & McDuffie Complts Sols.

Answer of defendants: In consequence of tender age they are incapable of judging their interests and submit to decree of Court. Whit Brooks, Guardian ad litem.

Samuel[?] Parker & Elizabeth Parker vs Geo Parker. Bill for sale of trust property. James Beams et al vs Harriet W Beams et al. Bill for sale of trust property.

Application to sell trust property. 4 Feby 1819 Whit Brooks has examined Edmund Bacon Esqr, Henry W Lowe, Doctr Wm Brazier & Hinchwill Mitchell trustee who concur that sale of property promotes interests provided the money be properly appropriated.

Decree. Question whether sale of trust property would be to advantage of parties; decision that it would be, and that Hinchall Mitchell one of trustees and Rebecca Beams be authorized to make titles; proceeds to be held by trustees; W Thompson, 5 Feby 1819.

#86   Armstead Burt & wife Mary late Mary Scott, Guardians, vs David Mims, Bill. [35 items] Armstead and Mary, guardians of Elizabeth Scott, John Scott, Samuel Scott, minor children of Samuel C Scott [paper torn] sd Armstead being guardian in right of his [paper torn] the wife of sd Samuel C [paper torn] who was the son of Samuel Scott, also deceased. That Samuel Scott [paper torn] ...ther, to Samuel C, grandfather to the wards of your complainants, being seized of considerable real and personal estate signed his will 21 January 1809 and after death of sd Samuel C Scott, thereby gave to sd children, wards of your orator and oratrix and grandchildren of sd Samuel Scott, three Negroes Hal, Amy and Judy. All his estate real and personal of which sd Samuel died seized should be sold, money arising from sale to be equally divided between his children and grandchildren, giving to Elizabeth Scott,

John Scott and Samuel the wards of your complainants an equal share with his children. Testator appointed George Graves, David Mims, and John Middleton executors. Testator died same year without revoking will. George Graves and John Middleton refusing to act, David Mims took possessions of sd deceased to amount of Six thousand nine hundred [blurred] five Dollars sixty five cents. Sold real estate. Oratrix, then Mary Scott, mother of Elizabeth, John, & Samuel was apptd their guardian on 13 June 1809. About 19 December past oratrix married orator whereby orator in right of his wife hath become entitled to legacies bequeathed to your complainants wards, as also to funds from sale of real estate and personal estate for benefit of your complainants wards. /s/ Armstead Burt, /s/ Mary Burt. 8 May 1812; Thos Meriwether J P. Financial evidence, 21 May 1819.

June 1819 Decree. Final settlement to be made; executor charged with interest on sums claimed by complts. Henry W DeSaussure.

#87   Executors of John Blocker vs Jane Cobb & others. Cross Bill. [16 items] Filed 25 January 1818. Juliany Blocker, James Blocker, John Blocker extx and extrs of will of John Blocker deed. Testator with Jane Cobb administered estate of James Cobb Jr decd. James OHarra & his wife Cynthia who are entitled to a distributive share of James Cobb's estate filed bill calling for accounting to them for their share of James Cobb's estate. James & Thomas Cobb have since been made parties to complainants Bill. State that John Blocker decd during course of his admn advanced to Jane Cobb, money & other articles for maintenance of children of James Cobb Jr decd amounting to $1379.04 after deducting [other] sums. Asks that Jane Cobb, James Cobb, Thomas Cobb, and James OHarrow & wife Cynthia answer complainants. Whit Brooks's accounting of sums advanced to admx. Answer of James Oharra, 3 Feby 1819; /s/ J Ohara. Jane Cobb and John Blocker decd took out Ltrs/ admn on estate of her deceased husband James Cobb Jr. She should be released from any subsequent expense attending final settlement of her husband's estate; she cannot even pretend to say account is incorrect, but submits same upon vouchers in complainants possession to decree of Court. Whatever was advanced to her by coadministrator in his lifetime went towards support of her children by her deceased husband which she prays may be taken as part of her answer and referred to in final settlement of his estate. Deft being ignorant of accounting cannot say whether she received from purchases at sale of her husband's estate more than her distributive share of same or whether she received due proportion of her part of the share which fell to her deceased daughter Sophronia but submits the same to Report of Commissioner and decree of Court. 20 Jany 1819; /s/ Janey Cobb. Parties agreed upon amt due from Dft to coadmr John Blocker for money advanced to her over & above her distributive share & further that the amt shall bear interest. If Mrs Cobb is credited on her acct with exrs of John Blocker with amt reported in her favour agt Jas Oharra & wife, then Mrs Cobb will stand indebted to sd exrs $2289.24. Whit Brooks C.E.E.D.

Accounts, estate of James Cobb, Mrs Jane Cobb admx, John Blocker admr: Daniel Marcus, Daniel Bird, S Tillman Esqr, M Blocker, J Blocker, Mrs Sneed, J Moore, Thos Cobb, Matt Mims, daughter Cinthia, Ab G Dozier, J & T Cobb, Thomas Cobb, McKenzie & Bennock, M Henry, your son John, A Sneed, J Campbell, N Sneed [part faded out]. John & James Blocker exrs in a/c with Mrs Jane Cobb & John S Cobb.

#88   James Blocker & wife Isabella M Blocker and George Miller & Anna B Miller his wife vs Samuel Marsh, guardian to wife & others. Bill for Relief. [11 items] In 1812 John Blocker Senr now deceased purchased of Daniel Mazyck land on Rockey Creek adj lands of James Miller. He covenanted that George Miller pay Mazyck half of purchase money and John Blocker would make title to Oratrix Anna B Miller for half of sd land. John Blocker verbally agreed that he would make title to other half to Isabella M Blocker when James Blocker paid other half of purchase money. Whole purchase money was paid by orators. John Blocker has since died and left following heirs: Juliana Blocker his widow, your orator James Blocker, John, Jesse, Abner, Barkely & David L Blocker his sons Benjamin Winn and Mary B his wife, also widow of Michael Blocker decd now married to Samuel Marsh, and children of sd Michael Blocker to wit Linnia, Julia, Adeline, & Jane Blocker of whom Samuel Marsh hath been appointed guardian by Court. Isabella and Anna desire title to their land.

Copy, will of James Blocker, 22 May 1831. Title to be made to land on Rocky Creek known as the Mazyck Tract with land adjoining known as Kittle tract to my wife Isabella M Blocker and my children for one half of same and title to Mrs Anna B Miller for other half. Name of John Blocker & Abner Blocker be stricken out as trustees in deed heretofore made for benefit of wife and children; name of B M Blocker inserted and he to act jointly with George Miller as trustee. Bird Tract where George Miller now lives purchased for George & wife. Half of tract on Clouds Creek to wife for benefit of herself and children. Titles to land on Beaverdam Creek of Clouds Creek; half of tract on Beaver Dam of Cuffeetown Creek; title to land in Spartanburg District on Fair Forest Creek; other half belongs to Genl Collins of Union Dist. /s/ James Blocker. Wit: James Bones, Moses Prescott, Ann E Morris.

Plat of 693 acres shows Rockey Creek, road from Edgefield Courthouse to Cambridge, and adj lands of James Williams, Hu Rose, William Mazyck, James Miller, Benjn Eddins, Silvanus Stevens. George Miller, Abner Blocker to Barkley Martin Blocker in trust for Isabella Morison Blocker. Filed 1818.

Order 5 Feby 1819 to executors of John Blocker decd make titles to complainants for lands in question, W Thompson, 5 Feby 1819.

#89   Comr Leroy Hammond vs Charles Goodwin. Bill to Foreclose. [15 items] Filed 19 April 1817. Sarah Quarles Hammond states that Leroy Hammond her late husband on 22 January 1802 made bond with Charles Goodwin Esqr for securing purchase money of land on Town Creek with mills thereon; land was purchased of John Star and John Prior exrs of will of John Prior decd millwright. Leroy Hammond became security for payment of purchase money for Charles Goodwin and signed bond with him. Charles Goodwin on 27 May 1806 executed counter security to Leroy Hammond, mortgaged land on Saluda and Green river; [many tracts mortgaged, lying on Saluda, Green, Enoree in Greenville, Little Edisto, Little Beaver Dam in Pendleton, Orangeburg District, Peters Point in Barnwell; names of Thomas Farrar and Col. Samuel Hammond mentioned.] Also mortgaged slaves: Big Corydoin, Sue, Sam, Dido, Pussey, Sally, Nero, Little Sue and her child Little Hannah, children of Dido, Prince, Berry, Poor Boy, and a male child of Amy's, Topaz, Coclia, Allick, Beason, Hannah, Joe, Will, Isaac child of Hannah, Jane & child Esther, Silla and child Harriet, Polydore, Moses, Stephen, Cloe, Loudoun, Augustus, Big Jim, Molly, Butler, Muster, Little Jim, Isaac, Primis & Cupid . Charles Goodwin took benefit of act for relief of insolvent debtors and assigned all his property for benefit of his creditors and James Beggs and Christian F Breithaupt are now selling, and Charles Goodwin assigned lands and Negroes above to them for benefit of creditors, subject of claims of Leroy Hammond. Leroy Hammond died 1818 intestate. Oratrix hoped Charles Goodwin would have paid John Star and John Prior and thereby released your oratrix from all liability, or that James Beggs & Christian T Breithaupt would have sold lands & negroes and settled the debt due to estate of John Prior the elder and others and thereby exonerated estate of Leroy Hammond from the same or else would have quietly and peaceably have delivered up possession to your oratrix of mortgaged premises.

#90   William Hall vs Richard Winn & wife & others. Filed 18 December 1817. [5 items] James Hall brother of orator died intestate without a child or widow, leaving as next of kin the children of Miles Hall who represent their deceased father who died before sd James Hall his brother and who reside in Virginia, Richard Winn who married Sally Hall sister of sd intestate residing in Virginia, Thomas Holloway resident of Georgia, John Holloway, Anderson Holloway, George Holloway, William Holloway resident in Edgefield District, and Elizabeth Poole widow of Mitchell Pool residence unknown, Edward Harrison and wife Mary, Nancy Holloway resident in Edgefield District, James Clary and his wife Martha child of George and Ann Holloway both deceased which Martha[Ann] was sister of sd intestate James Hall and which sd George and Martha died intestate before death of James Hall, Patsy Hall resident in Virginia, Richard Hall, Thomas Hall resident in Edgefield Sistrict, John Francis Samson and Eliza Hall resident in Edgefield children of John and Sally Hall which sd John Hall was brother of sd James Hall who survived his brother and who together with his wife died intestate. John Wall and wife Amy the latter is another sister of James Hall the intestate. Armstead Hall residence unknown brother of intestate James Hall, Thomas Hall another brother of sd intestate resident in Sumpter District, John Lenoir and wife Lucy another sister of sd intestate resident in Sumpter District, and Prudence Goudy another sister of sd James Hall deceased, and your orator brother of intestate James Hall decd. James died possessed of considerable real and personal estate the later of which has been legally divided or is subject to division. Two tracts of land remain. Division of land impracticable; asks sale.

#91   Solomon Lucas vs John Roebuck, Ezekiel Roebuck and others. Injunction & Relief. [3 items] [This suit appears to be missing a first page] Ann Green and her husband died leaving John Green, Silas Green, William Green, Coclia Green since married to Isaac Hopkins, Frances Green since married to Saunders Day their heirs in law. Orator is without remedy except by Court of Equity. [illegible line at fold of paper] James Roebuck, Isaac Hopkins and wife Coclia, James Day and wife Betsey, John Hardy and wife Clara, Daniel Hardy and wife Polly shall account for the share of John Roebuck's estate which they have received and untill your orator shall have opportunity of obtaining indemnification from the estate of John Roebuck, Ezekiel Roebuck [blank] William Nichols [blank] and that John Roebuck [fold of paper] James Roebuck, Polly Roebuck, John Green, Silas Green, William Green, Isaac Hopkins, Saunders Day, William Cannon, James Day, Benjamin Roebuck, John Hardy and Daniel Hardy may set forth which real property John Roebuck decd possessed and the value thereof and refund to your orator the money which he has been obliged to pay on account of sd John Roebuck and pay the amount of the said execution. Saunders Day is now in possession of a tract of land of 213 acres. /s/ Solomon (x) Lucas. 6 February 1813; Wm Hagins JP. Injunction issued to stay proceedings. W Thompson. 11 Feby 1813.

#92   Susanna Rambo and others v George Hancock, John Allen and others. Bill for injunction & relief [25 items] Filed 13 Apr 1811. Injunction issued April 1811; Henry Wm DeSaussure. [Second order too dark to read on microfilm]. Susanna Rambo, Mary Moore Rambo, Martha S Rambo, Reuben James Rambo, Matilda Elizabeth Rambo, Albert Jefferson Rambo, Augustus Bardwin Rambo, sue by next friend and natural guardian Susanna Rambo. Joseph Rambo was seized of 112 acres on Foxes Creek of Savannah River. Rambo's intemperance threatened to ruin his family. [Susanna and her mother Mary Daley took measures to secure Susanna and family from consequences of Joseph's extravagant habit by Mary's providing money to have land bought by James McQueen for benefit of Susanna and children; taking from Joseph the power to sell it.] Oratrix had no fraudulent intention in sd transaction. Joseph Rambo at that time owed only a small sum due on judgment amounting to about $100. James McQueen never had possession of sd land and allowed Joseph & your oratrix & family to retain possession. James McQueen offered land for sale. John Hall purchased it. James McQueen informed oratrix he had purchased land; Susanna has remained in possession. James McQueen died intestate leaving Ann McQueen, Peter McQueen, Caroline McQueen and William McQueen his heirs. George Hancock administered estate which proved insufficient to pay demands against it. Joseph Rambo died in August 1809 leaving widow and children. Susanna Rambo offered to pay James McQueen for expences he incurred during the different transactions; has made similar offers to George Hancock, admr, both refused. George Hancock confederated how to defraud Susanna & family of their claims to the land. John Allen asks to be made a party to this bill, about to force a sale as property of James MCQueen at public outcry. /s/ Susannah Rambo. John Lyon QU. 5 Ap 1811.

Answer of George Hancock guardian of Ann McQueen, Peter McQueen, Caroline McQueen, & William Henry McQueen infants under age twenty one. The land in question is the only property now belonging to the estate of their Father; infants submit to judgment of the Court. /s/ George Hancock, 22 May 1812; S Butler C.C.P.

Answer of George Hancock, admr estate of James McQueen. Did not understand from intestate that contract existed between Susanna Rambo or Mary Daley and James McQueen. Intestate after purchase at sheriffs sale of land in dispute, went upon premises and in presence of dft exerted acts of ownership, built two houses near to dwelling where Joseph and Susannah Rambo resided. They were present. Neither objected. Knows nothing of promise made by James McQueen that it was bought for person other than himself. Joseph Rambo considered himself tenant of James McQueen after afsd foreclosure. 22 May 1812; S Butler CCP

Answer of John C Allen to Leroy Hammond & others. Land mentioned was sold at sheriffs sale under execution at suit of Thomas Garrett against Joseph Rambo while this dft was sheriff of Edgefield Dist. Tract was purchased by John Hall as agent of James McQueen and, as dft was informed by letter from James McQueen at time of sale and by himself personally, for Susanna Rambo now Susanna Hammond; also for benefit of Susanna's children by Joseph Rambo. Land sold for $125, $100 of which was paid by John Hall, balance by James McQueen. When titles were executed by dft to James McQueen, dft was informed by James McQueen that all purchase money for sd land was paid by Susanna Rambo & that he had purchased the land merely as her agent & for benefit of her & children. Joseph Rambo & family lived on sd land at the time of sale & Susanna and her children continued to live thereon after Joseph's death untill her marriage to Leroy Hammond. Dft understood sd land was purchased for benefit of Susanna and children to prevent it from being confiscated by wasteful extravagance of Joseph Rambo who was addicted to drinking and was likely to reduce his family to begging. /s/ John C Allen. Barnwell District. John C Allen made oath as to truth. 11 March 1812; John Carr J P. George Hancock et al ads Leroy Hammond et al. Edmund Bacon under impression that the Court embraced testimony of Benjamin Grumbles. Propounds interrogation questions. Commissioners John R Bartee, Joseph Fuller Jr, John Torrence. Promissory notes, James McQueen to Joseph Rambo and William Pond. Letter from McQueen to Mrs Rambo. Land bought for McQueen at Sheriff sale by John Hall for me. 12 Sept 1807. Deed, Sheriff John C Allen to James McQueen, 24 June 1807. Wit Wilson Woodroof, John James. Proved 27 October 1808, Wilson Woodroof.

William Hall vs Richard Winn. Many of defendants, children of Miles Hall, Richard Winn, Thomas Holloway, Elizabeth Poole, Patcy Hall, Armstead Hall reside out of State, they are given three months to plead from the publication of this notice in Richmond Enquirer. Mary Snead et al vs Jane Cobb & others. Mary Hart, Cecilia Hart, Claiborne...
[no second page]

#93 Meredith William Moon & David Bates vs Sarah Smith, Stephen Herndon and others. Bill for Relief. [145 items] [discolored; abstract may be inexact]. Moon, guardian of minor Andrew Lee Lark, only son and heir of Cullin Lark & wife Nancy, heir of Andrew Lee decd, and David Bates & wife Sarah late Sarah Lee daughter & devisee of Andw Lee. Andrew Lee died Dec 1795 leaving widow Nancy Lee, daughter Susannah who about six years after married Stephen Herndon, Hannah who had previously married Lewis Patrick, Nancy Lee afterwards mother of your orator M W Moon, and Sarah Lee wife of your orator David Bates lately married, and sons John W Lee, Gersham Lee, and Wilson Lee. Andrew Lee left Nancy Lee his widow and his daughter Susannah Lee executrixes and Jacob Smith executor, all qualified. Jacob Smith returned appraisement and inventory 8 March 1796 which omits debts due estate & testate's sums in hand. His having cash was notorious, his bridge and mill on the Saluda river independent of the plantation were constant sources of income. Jacob Smith must have received large sums, particularly before the marriage of Susannah yet the inventory is the only return Jacob made. Nancy Lee, executrix, made no return; after Susannah Lee's marriage Stephen Herndon (principal dft) and Jacob Smith managed estate, Stephen as exr in right of wife. Jacob made no return; only account of sales returned by Stephen was 24 February 1806, extended from Oct 1797 to Jan 1803, and partial sales of Gersham Lee's estate. Only accounts current returned by Stephen purports to have been made out by Susannah. Nancy Lee, intending marriage with [blank] Vaughn and to prevent him from possessing slaves purchased by Nancy Lee, a breeding wench Jude and her daughter Phillis, gave them to Susannah. Stephen and John W should give equal value to the younger children of Andrew Lee when they should arrive at full age which they have not done. Orators heard Stephen Herndon has been making returns to Ordinary of Newberry District relating to Andrew Lee's estate. Stephen went to improper office; peculiar situation of Ordinary for Newberry District afforded inducement.

West Tennessee, Lincoln Co, Septr 17, 1815, Nathl Norwood recollects he carried money for Jacob Smith, gave it to Sheriff Sampson Butler, gave receipt to Mr Smith. It was money from Mr Herndon that married Susannah Lee that was to defray cost on some suit; stated that Mr Butler had been at his house a few days before he received the money from Mr Herndon. Doesn't recollect paying any other money for Mr Smith.

Lewis Patrick, deft, wife Hannah Lee received due proportion of Andrew Lee's estate, Lewis Patrick gave bond to Stephen Herndon that he had received his full part.

Jacob Smith died 1806 leaving a large estate, his wife Sarah Smith extx, his son Luke Smith extr. Luke having died, Sarah is defendant to this bill as surviving representative of that estate and also of the estate of Andrew Lee decd, she having duly qualified as extx.

Gersham Lee died 23 October 1802; was anxious to give his estate to the two younger children, Wilson and Sarah, made will. Gersham was not of age by ten days, he requested that no advantage be taken on that account. Stephen Herndon and wife and John W Lee assented, Herndon giving bond in approbation of agreement, but no sooner had Gersham breathed his last, than Susannh Herndon, finding will had no legacy for her,committed it to the flames. Gersham Lee died worth nearly $2000 besides mill and hands devised to him. On 25 March 1806 John W Lee took out ltrs of admn on Gersham's estate. Only paper relating to Gershams estate ever returned to the proper office by John W Lee is an inventory of one Negro slave appraised at $245 [more accusations of financial corruption]

Reply of George Lewis Patrick sworn 27 May 1814; Wm Spragins JP. Reply of Jno W Lee 11 May 1815. Will of Gersham Lee 23 October 1802, wit Drury T Vaughn, James Vaughn. To brother Wilson Lee one equal half of my grist mill, 250 acres acres adj mill; To sister Sarah Lee my mill. To brother John Lee other half of grist mill and 250 acres adj mill. To sister Hannah Patrick eldest son Lewelling Patrick Negro man Tom, to sister Sarah Lee Negro girl Silvia, to brother and sister Wilson and Sarah Lee my part of my father's property. Appoint Nicholas Vaughn and Stephen Herndon executors. 23 October 1802. /s/ Gersham Lee. Wit Drewry T Vaughn, James Vaughn. Answer of Stephen Herndon. Accounts. Report of Whitfield Brooks, Commissioner 7 Jan 1817. [Testimony is too discolored to read] Stephen Herndon is indebted to the estate. The commr states the estimated sum extravagant and much above the actual sum, 1816 [month and day obliterated]. Answer of John W Lee dft to charge of Andrew Lee Lark by gdn William Meredith Moon and David Bates and wife.

Wilson Lee's nuncupitive will 11 January last. We Henry Domanick Senr, Marget Domanick and Agnes Domanick present. Wished his sister Sarah Bates to have his whole estate. Jacob Bates JP. Sworn 5 June 1813. Confirmed 24 June 1813 by John Simkins, Ordinary. Sworn David Bates executor 29 June 1813.

Decree signed by William Dobin James, Henry Wm DeSaussure, Thomas Waties, Court of Appeals, 16 Decr 1816.

#94 John Middleton vs Wm Olds and others. Bill for Discovery & Relief. [33 items] Samuel Scott purchased of William Stanton negro Sam who remained in his possession untill his death on 1 February 1809. Scott bequeathed Sam to his daughter Elizabeth Middleton previously married to Orator who obtained possession of Sam in right of his wife and kept Sam untill 13 October 1812 when Sam was seized by Enoch Howard for William W Olds to satisfy to mortgage of Sam said to have been given by William Stanton together with seven other slaves to John Campbell and John Nielson of Augusta, Georgia, to secure $1433.48 with interest from 1April 1806. Mortgage recorded in Wilkes County, Georgia. Campbell and Nielson did not claim Negroes: allowed Wm Stanton to retain possession from 1 April 1806 untill 19 May 1807, allowing him to sell them as his own property. Samuel Scott remained in possession of Sam; after his death your orator untill Sam was seized by order of William W Olds. Orator is convinced that if Samuel Scott had known of mortgage he never would have purchased Sam and given $500 for him. He was notoriously cautious in his dealings. August 1812 /s/ John Middleton. [Also copy 8 February 1817, certified by Whit Brooks, Cr EED.]

Answer of William W Olds. John and William Stanton were indebted to Campbell and Nielson of Georgia, and mortgaged Negroes. On 13 October 1812 in order to foreclose, levied on Sam, then in possession of complainant. Sam was taken to courthouse and publickly sold after due notice when defendant purchased him for $280, paid to sheriff James Butler. On same day dft sold Sam to John Traylor. Dft knows nothing of the way Middleton came by Sam. 14 Feby 1816, /s/ Wm W Olds.

Will of Samuel Scott. Daughter Sarah Mims, daughter Mary Graves Moore, daughter Elisabeth Middleton, grandchildren Elisabeth Scott, John Scott, Samuel Scott, daughter and sons of Samuel G Scott decd. Grandson John Allen Scott Martin. Exrs George Graves, David Mims, John Middleton. Wit John Boyd, James Bunt, Mary Scott. 21 January 1809. Copy certified 4 June 1816, Jn Simkins OED.

Indenture 1 April 1806, Georgia, William Stanton and John Stanton of Wilkes County, and John Campbell and John Nielson of Augusta. Mortgage: Armstead age 23, Sam 28, Bob 35, Will 14, Dinah 29, Jenney 11, Nancy 12. Wit Wm Bones, Joseph B Stanton.

Decree: Wm W Olds who had married with Stanton's daughter, gave his children the mortgaged negroes except Sam. Scott was an innocent purchaser. Sam to be delivered to complainant, and if cannot be found, purchase money and hire to be paid to complainant, and dft pay costs of suit. W Thompson. Receipt of Wm Stanton for Samuel Scott's purchase of Sam $500, 19 May 1807; Wit John Middleton.

#95 Daniel Matthews and Martha Matthews widow of Moses Matthews vs Hardy Matthews, Micajah Matthews and others. Bill for partition. [25 items] In behalf of Martha's under age children: [Enoch Matthews, Mary Matthews were written and crossed through], Budeade Matthews, William Matthews, and Eleanor Matthews; also in behalf of William Hardy and Anna his wife late Anna Matthews, Jacob Pope and Elizabeth his wife late Elizabeth Matthews and Daniel Carrinton and Cabel his wife late Cabel Matthews, children of Martha and Moses Matthews decd, all except Budcade and Cabel of Ninety Six District. 25 March 1791 Isaac Matthews died leaving widow Anna Matthews now decd and sons Moses, Lewis, Hardy, Micajah, your Orator Daniel, and daughters Cabell who married Thomas Pace now deceased and since married Benjamin Cox of Georgia, and Elizabeth Matthews married George Fluker resident in Ninety Six District. Isaac left estate of original grant to William Whitaker 4 October 1768, 250 acres on Little Saluda adj at time of survey by William West, but 525 acres according to resurvey by John Blocker the younger Esqr. Land was conveyed by Whitaker to John Chesnut Esqr of Camden; purchased of him jointly by Isaac Matthews and his son Moses Mathis, eldest son of Isaac & late husband of your Oratrix Martha Matthews for one hundred pounds, equal proportion of which Isaac and Moses paid to John Chesnut, although titles were made to Isaac Matthews alone, under agreement that half of land was to secure to Moses as his property. It was dying wish of Isaac Matthews that half of land should become property of Daniel Matthews. After Isaac's death, Orator's brothers Moses, Lewis, Hardy, and Micajah being anxious to shew that their father's estate had been settled in peace, entered entered into agreement in writing certifying that five brothers Moses, James, Hardy, Micajah, and Daniel made bond five hundred pounds sterling to consent 31 December 1798 sale of Negroes Anthony and Peter, and four brothers Moses, James, Hardy and Micajah agreed to give titles to part of land to our brother Daniel Matthews. Orator and oratrix kept possession, but tract has never been partitioned. Moses died leaving your oratrix his widow and children afsd. Lewis Matthews has also died leaving widow Nancy Matthews since married with Bailey Crouch but having with Lewis children Elizabeth married Thomas Waits by whom she had one child Nancy and died leaving child a minor; also Shugar Jones Matthews, Cabel Matthews, Mary Quarles Matthews, Moses Matthews, Josiah Allen Matthews, Drury Matthews, and Milberry Matthews, all sd children are now under age except the first, which renders it impossible to make good title to sd land.

Hardy Matthews, George Fluker and wife, Micajah Matthews, Benjamin Carr & Cabel his wife, Bailey Couth[?] and Nancy his wife in behalf of [illeg] and Sugar Abney, Cabel Mary Quarles, Moses Josiah Allen Drury & Milberry [paper torn] and Thomas Wait in behalf of himself and his minor child Nancy Wait defendants ads Daniel Matthews, Martha Matthews & others. Think plaintiffs prayer reasonable and have no objection to partition of sd land and that titles be made as plfs request. Call upon Court to make titles.

Daniel Matthews is entitled to one half; Moses Matthews was entitled to the other half and since his death his legal heirs are entitled to their half to wit Martha Matthew widow of Moses to one third part of one half and Jacob Pope in behalf of his wife, William Hardy in right of his wife, Daniel Carrinton in right of his wife, Arthur Fort in right of his wife, and Enoch Matthews, Budcade Matthews, William Matthews, and Eleanor Matthews are entitled to the remaining two thirds of half of sd land in equal proportions, that is to say one eighth part and they pray this court good titles to be made to them. Order to Sampson Pope, Aaron Etheridge, David Bates, Sampson Wilson and William Fluker appraise land. Recommend that land be sold. Whitfield Brooks, 5 June 1815. /s/ Sampson Wilson /s/ D Bates /s/ Wm Fluker, /s/ Aaron Ethridge, 17 June 1815.

#96 William Mays Guardian of Anna Whitley a minor, the daughter and one of the surviving children of Stephen Whitley deceased vs Anna Whitley and others. Bill of Discovery, Relief. [15 Items] Filed 26 July 1816. Stephen Whitley died intestate 180 Possessed of property and leaving a small family all of whom are deceased except Anna and one other child. Stephen's father John Whitley administered estate. John died leaving will, his wife Anna Whitley and his son Lewis Whitley executors. Stephen's estate has not paid what is due Mays as guardian. Anna Whitley, Lewis Whitley and William Whitley do not make disclosure of estate to Mays.

Subpoena to Anna Whitley, Lewis Whitley and William Whitley. 26 July 1816

26 October 1807 sale of property of Stephen Whitley. Buyers William Abney Junr, John Holloday Junr, William Dodgen, Daniel Rogers, James Wray, Caleb Holloway, John Williams, Phillip Hazel, Matthew Mays, Manrisig Towls, William Carter Junr, Elizabeth Thompson, Christopher Kohnily, John Blaylock Junr, John Blaylock, Matthew Wray, John Towls, John Whitley Senr, William Carter Senr, John Bledsoe, Jeremiah Wilson, Gardner Mays, Edmund Wray, William Adams, James Thompson, Thomas Scurry, Reuben Taylor, William Baird, William Scurry, Edmund May, Isaac Saddler, Tabitha Deen, Simon Baird, James House, Edey Baker, Syntha Burnham, Phillip Shug, Jordan Holloway, Nathan Baker, Nathaniel Abney, Henry Weaver, Robert Bryan, Bennet Hancock, Elizabeth Whitley, William Bearden, John Ross, Lewis Fowler, Abraham Rayleigh, Nathan Abney Junr, John Hardy, Thomas Morriss, Joseph Mays, William Carter, John Whitley.

#97   Agatha Middleton widow of Hugh Middleton decd agst Richard Quarles and wife Sally, Alexander Colhoun Hamilton & wife Delphia Adelia, William Tennent & wife Patsey, Elizabeth Middleton, Samuel Savage & wife, William Middleton minor by S Savage his guardian, John Middleton & Stephen Garrett.   Cross Bill for discovery & Partition. 15 September 1809. [9 items] Sally and Delphia Adelia, daughters of Agatha's late husband, filed bill of complaint against oratrix. Stephen Garrett and John Middleton coadmrs with your oratrix of estate of her decd husband. Sd John Middleton is also son of her late husband. Patsey is also daughter of sd husband against Elizabeth Middleton another of her husband's daughters and also against Samuel Savage who married Milly Middleton widow of Hugh Middleton junior decd and guardian of William Middleton a minor son of Hugh Middleton junior who was son of her late husband. In sd bill they state that her late husband was seized of estate of inherited lands in Edgefield and elsewhere of great value also of personal estate, leases. He died intestate leaving oratrix his widow, Mary Middleton afterwards Mary Findley his daughter and Sally wife of Richard Quarles both daughters by his second wife; after her death he married Lucy Williams by whom he had Hugh who died before his father leaving his only child, William. Also children of her late husband John, Patsey, Elizabeth and Delphia Adelia. After death of oratrix's husband Mary married Edward Findley. First she and her then husband died intestate and without issue. Richard Quarles had administered on both their estates and the court had appointed Samuel Savage guardian of William Middleton grandson of your orator's husband. [Asks Court to discover and account for personal effects and lands already given by oratrix's late husband to some of his children, and that the remaining part of the estate be divided according to law.]

#98   Thomas Adkinson, guardian to Whitfield Brown, vs James Carson, Bill for Account & Relief. [13 items] Filed 27 July 1820. George Brown, father of complainant's ward, died leaving a small estate whereof Whitfield is entitled to a distributive share. James Carson three or four years ago while Whitfield was under age 14 was guardian and obtained Whitfield's portion of the personal property, $1300. Whitfield at age 16 or 17 has chosen Adkinson his guardian. Says property is insecure. Asks that James give account of his guardianship, believe Carson indebted to Brown.

Affidavit of Thos Adkinson, 27 July 1820.

Report of Whitfield Brooks, 8 June 1821. James Carson, former guardian, is indebted to sd minor Whitfield Brown $1317.92 including interest down to 1 January 1821 and also interest on $1113.49 from 1 January 1821 till paid.

#99   Joseph Eddings & wife Elizabeth, Rachel Mitchell, Starling Mitchell, Joseph Calders[?] and wife Elizabeth, and Samuel Walker surviving trustee for Rebecca Beams, Rebecca Beams and James Beams her husband vs William B Mays, Bill for Partition. [9 items] Complainants say Samuel Walker Senr died seized of land on Horns Creek that by his will July [line lost in crease of paper] his daughter Anna now the wife of William Mays and his daughter Sarah who married Chaney Farrow and is now dead leaving husband and [blank] her children her representatives, Martha J Walker is willing to relinquish her claim to sd land. Ask land be sold for partition.

Benjamin Frazier, William Robertson & William Johnson state land cannot be divided without injury to someone of the heirs. 4 June 1821. Order of sale, John Garrett & others v

John Day & others.
Madison County, Alabama 14 April 1821, relinquishment of dower by Martha J Walker, widow of Samuel Walker deceased. Witnesses Samuel Walker, Benjamin Holloway. Will of Samuel Walker, father-in-law of William B Mays. Negroes to be purchased in five years for daughters Sarah, Anna both between age of 16 and 20, the other three to be about 7 or 8 years. For grandchildren Martha, Samuel and Benjamin Holloway. Witness Samuel Marsh, John Ryan, James Head. /s/ Saml Walker. Copy ceritified 3 March 1821 by Jno Simkins. Petition granted 4 June 1821, Whit Brooks C^r E E D

#100   Nicholas Delaigle of Augusta, Georgia, vs Jos Carrie. Bill to Foreclose mortgage. [7 items] Dft ackd service & became a party to this suit 5 Oct 1820. Order granted 28 January 1821. Whit Brooks. Joseph Carrie late of Augusta but now of Beach Island, South Carolina. Nicholas endorsed several notes of hand in bank of City of Augusta provided Joseph would give him indemnity against payments he might have to make. Mortgaged land 30 April 1819. [list of notes] also Negroes: Peter, Hannah, Simon and his wife Sealy, Aggy and future increase of females.
Decree, Negroes to be sold by sheriff; mortgage foreclosed. W Thompson, 5 Feby 1821.

INDEX

BEAVERDAM CREEK, 49 60
BEAVINS, Jas 6
BEDDINGFIELD, John 3
BEGGS, James 60-61
BELL, Harrison 2 James 47 Peggy 30
   Samuel 30-31
BENDER, Geo 14 George 1 13 Mary
   Ann 13 20 Mrs 19 Polly 20 Sarah 13
BENNET, 42
BENNETT, Hudson 42
BENNING, Pleasant 11
BENNOCK, 59
BESELY, Sarah 7
BETTIS, Francis 6 Jesse 4
BEVANS, 20
BIG HORSE CREEK, 29-30
BILBO, James 7 57
BILL, Cross 2
BIRD, Daniel 36 52 59 Elijah 45
BITTLE, Rebecca 8
BLALOCK, H 52 Harden 3 29 48 Jno
   30 Margaret 29 Millington 57 Sarah
   57
BLAND, P 38 Presly 37-38 W B 37
BLAYLOCK, John 66 John Jr 66
BLEDSOE, John 66
BLEDSOW, Levi 38
BLOCKER, Ab 6 Abner 4 27 44 60
   Adaline 44 Adeline 60 Anna 60 B M
   60 Barkely 60 Barley Martin 60
   Benjamin Winn 60 David L 60
   Isabella M 59-60 Isabella Morison
   60 J 59 James 44 53 59-60 Jane 60
   Jas 51 Jesse 6 45 47 60 John 32 50
   52-53 59-60 65 John Sr 52 60 Julia
   44 60 Juliana 53 60 Juliany 53 59
   Lavinia 44 Linnia 60 M 59 Mary B
   60 Michael 44 54 60
BLUNDELL, William 38
BOATRIGHT, Celia 6-7
BOATWRIGHT, Celia 5
BOLTON, John 20
BONDHAM, Milldge L 38
BONES, 47 James 60 Wm 65
BONHAM, Elizabeth Jemima 37 James
   37-38 42 James Butler 37 John Whit
   37 John Whitiel 38 Malicha 37
   Millie Lucke 37 Mrs 38

BONHAM(cont.)
   Rachel Juliana 37 Sarah Mary 38
   Simeon Smith 37 Sophia 37-38
BONNET, 41
BOOKS, Whitfield 53
BOOSH, Richard 54
BORU, 14
BOSTICK, Davis 24 Test Washington
   44 Tolaver 24 44 Toliver 24
   Washington 24 William 24 Willis 24
BOWEN, George 45
BOWERS, B 2-3 Ben 2 Benjamin 1-3
   Benjm 3 Benjmain 2 Benjn 2 David
   1-2 8 David Jr 2 David Sr 2 Giles 1-2
   14 20 Mary 2 Sarah 1-2
BOWIE, George 46
BOXIE, 14
BOYD, Ezekiah 22 H K 22 Henry K 22
   John 16 21-22 65 John Jr 22 W E 22
BOZEMAN, Harman W 18 Harmon 8
   Nancy 18
BRACKET, Mrs 19
BRACKETT, John 20
BRANSON, Elenor 30 Eli 30 Mary 30
   Thomas 30
BRANWELL DISTRICT, 20
BRAZER, William 18
BRAZIEL, Wm 53
BRAZIER, Wm 58
BREITHAUPT, 40 C 57 Christian 40
   Christian F 60 Christian S 29
   Christian T 61 Christn 39
BRENAN, E 41 Eugene 19 42
BRIDGES, Ohn 42
BRIGS, Henry 53
BRISTOL GREAT BRITAIN, 36
BROAD PATH, 38
BROOKS, James 42 Mr 16 W 8 10
   Whit 3 5-8 10-14 16 18 21 24 31 33
   35-36 38 44-54 56-59 65 68
   Whitefield 51 Whitfield 1 6 8-9 31
   47 49 51 64 66-67 Y S 31 Zach S 52
   Zachariah S 52
BROWN, Catharine 29 George 67
   James 29-30 Jane 29 John 6 Martha
   50 Swan J 50 Whitfield 67
BRUNELL, Craddock 13
BRUNER, Daniel 8 Mary 8 Michael 8

BRUNER (cont.)
Rebecca 8 Sally 8
BRYAN, Elisha 16 Robert 66 William
Tobler 16
BRYANT, Elisha 15 William 15
BUFFINGTON, Henry 55 Hester 55
James 55 Joseph 55 Matilda 55 Polly
55-56 Richard 55 Richd 56 Tilly 55
BUGG, Edmd 6 N H 12
BUIST, James 16
BUKHALTER, John 45
BULL, William 37 Wm 2 38
BULL SLUICE, 22
BULLOCK, Duke M 43-44 Eliza C 43
Elizabeth A 44 George W 43 George
Washington 44 J 43 James A 43-44
John 43-44 John W 43-44 Joseph M
43-44 Lucinda 44 Lucinda A 43
Rebecca 43-44 Rebecca W 43
Richard 52 William P 43 Wm P 44
BUNCE, William J 12
BUNT, James 65
BUR---, Jeremiah 54
BURCH, Richard 40
BURCKHALTERS CREEK, 57
BURDETT, Wm 38
BURGESS, Cresey 46 John 8 Saml 14
Samuel 8
BURKE COUNTY GEORGIA, 20
BURNELL, Craddock 3 13 Cradk 1
Cradock 1-2 34 36
BURNETT, Anthony 54-55 Benjamin
54 Catharine 54 Eliz 54 57 Elizabeth
54-55 57 Elizabeth M 57 Hezekiah
54-55 Isaac 55 57 Jeremiah 54-55 57
Jeremiah Sr 57 Katharine 55
Luvanna 57 Marian 57 Martin 57
Mary 18 Nancy 18-19 Polly 19
Robert 54-55 Robt 54 Sanders 54
Thom 18 Thomas 18-19 54-55 57
Thomas Jr 18 Thos 19 54 William
18-19 54-55
BURNEY, Mary 12-13 Mrs 13 20 Polly
19 William 13-14 19
BURNHAM, Syntha 66
BURT, Armstead 12 22 58-59 Mary 58-
59 Wm 56
BURTON, Robt 42

BUSSEY, Dempsey 18 George 47
Jeremiah 12
BUTLER, 45 48 Andrew 33-34 Andrew
P 27 Bld 50 Elizabeth S 31 Geo 6
George 31 James 6 38 65 Jas M 52
Jno R 31 John 8 John R 31 Joseph 1
14 Leontine 50 Mr 63 Nancy 31 S 62
Samp 6 Sampson 31 52 54 63
Stanmore 31 Tho 42 Thomas 24
Thos 37 William M 31 Wm 1 50
CAIN, William 42
CALDERS, Elizabeth 67 Joseph 67
CALDWELL, 47 John 20
CALHOUN, Alexr 29 Catharine 29
CALLIHAM, Eliza 22 Mrs 22
CAMBRIDGE, 10 60
CAMBRIDGE ABBEVILLE
DISTRICT, 44
CAMBRIDGE COMMONS, 44
CAMMACK, Robert 19
CAMPBELL, J 59 John 6 64-65
CAMPBELLTON, 23 36
CAMPLACE, John 20
CANFIELD, John 43
CANNON, J 6 William 61 Winifred 28
Winney 28
CANTELOU, L 32 Lewis 20 31-32
Louis 31
CARKIN, John C Jr 36
CARLILE, Elisabeth 3 Francis 3
CARLISLE, Elizabeth 1 Francis 1
CARLOSS, Amelia W 6
CAROLINA, 40
CARPENTER, Dennis 6 Denny 7
CARR, Benjamin 66 Cabel 66 John 63
Joshua 56
CARRIE, Jos 68 Joseph 68
CARRINTON, Cabel 65 Daniel 65-66
CARSON, James 56 67 Sarah 52
CARSTAFFIN, Mr 20
CARTER, Charles 34 Jacob 35 William
66 William Jr 66 William Sr 66
CARVEY, Thomas 6
CARY, Mary 45-46 Mrs 46
CASON, Larkin 56
CATFISH CREEK, 31
CAULEY, Catht 11
CAULK, Peter 56

CAVIACH, Edward 42
CHARLESTON, 10 20 23 36 38
CHENEY, John 7
CHEROKEE PONDS, 22
CHESNUT, John 65
CHILES, Thomas 44
CHRISTIAN, Thos 6
CHRISTMAS, Richard 45
CHRISTY, Robert 24
CLAR, Mary 55
CLARK, Aaron 51 Abner 55-56 David
   54 Jno 13 John 1-2 12 John Jr 8
   Nancy 51 Patcy 55 Patsey 55
   Susannah 56 Thomas 22
CLARKE, Aaron 51 Abner 55
   Catherine 51 Eleanor 13 Helena 20
   Henry 55 James 51 Jno 14 John 1 13-
   14 19-20 John Jr 8 35 Leonard 51
   Mary 55-56 Molly 55 Mrs 56 Nancy
   51 Patcy 55 Polly 55 Thomas 51
   Thos 51 William Rice 42
CLARY, James 61 Martha 61
CLEVELAND, John 18
CLEVELING, Jamy 6
CLEVLING, Jacob 6
CLICOLING, James 7
CLOUDS CREEK, 60
COALTER, Daniel 29
COBB, Barbara 52-53 Cynthia 52-53
   Eliza 53 Elizabeth 52 J 59 James 52-
   53 59 James Jr 59 Jane 39 52-53 59
   63 Janey 59 John 6 53 John S 52-53
   59 Jude 53 Mrs 53 59 Sophronia 59
   Sophrony 52 T 59 Thomas 12 18 52-
   53 59 Thomas Sr 52-53 Thos 27 59
   Thos Sr 53
COBBS, James 53 Janey 53 Thomas 54
COGBURN, D 21 David 14 20-21
   James 14 Martha 14 William 14
COLEMAN, Reuben 52 William 50 52
COLLIER, Edwd 37 Joseph 54
COLLINS, Genl 60 Horatio 8 Sally 8
COLUMBIA, 19 28 31 38
COLUMBIA COLLEGE, 4
COLUMBIA GEORGIA, 2
COLVIN, Daniel 29 Danl 29
COMES, Nathaniel 44
CONNER, Catlett 43

COOK, Amanda 11-12 Burwell 41
   Carolina 11 Caroline 11 John 10-11
   Martha 11 Mary 40-41 Nathan 40-42
   Polly 10 Prudence 11 Robt Z 11
   Sally 11 Susannah 41 W 12 West 10-
   12 19
COOPER, George H 56 Mrs 56
   Nicholas 19 54
COPHER, Harmon 11
CORLEY, Abner 42 John 42
COSPER, Harman 56 Henry 56
COTTON, Samuel 42
COUDREY, John 42
COULD, Reuben 6
COURSEY, Wm 47
COUTH, Bailey 66 Nancy 66
COWDREY, J M 46
COWES, Martha 44 Nathaniel 44
COX, Benjamin 65 Cabell 65
   Christopher 11 Cornelius 57 James
   56 John M 6 Joseph 2 Nancy 57
   William 11
COY, William 42
CRAFTON, Saml 27
CRANE, James 45
CRAVEN, Nancy 5
CRAVEN COUNTY, 39
CRAWFORD, 58 Charles 40 David 32
CROUCH, Bailey 66 Nancy 66
CUFFEE TOWN CREEK, 52
CUFFEETOWN CREEK, 31-32 46-47
   52 60
CULLIN, Nancy 63
CUMBOA, 29-30
CUMBOA'S MILL, 29-30
CUN-NINGHAM, Polly 24
CUNELL, James 56
CUNNINGHAM, Catharine 24-25 Caty
   26 James 26 Jno 41 John 24-27 Jose
   24-26 Joseph 25-26 Mrs 26 Polley
   26-27 Polly 24-27 William 24-26
CURRIE, Nebuchadnezar 34
CURRY, Cader 19 John 29
CUSHMAN, Simeon 1 3
D'ARNIELLE, I Anselm 40 Isaac 40
DALEY, Mary 62
DARBY, Benj 20 Benjamin 14 20
   Benjn 20-21 James 20-21

DARBY (cont.)
Martha 20-21 William 20-21
DARNIELLE, Elizabeth 40 Isaac 40
DAVIS, Chely 42 James Jr 42 James Sr
42 Maryan Williams 42 Samuel 42
Terry 42
DAY, Betsey 61 Elizabeth 28 Frances
28 61 James 28-29 61 John 29 50 68
Sanders 28-29 Saunders 28 61 Willm
29
DEAN, Catherine 51 William 51
DEEN, John 52 Tabitha 66 William 42
DEFTS, Jeter 49
DELAIGLE, Nicholas 68
DELEVIS, Henriette Charlotte 39
Therese Gabrielle 39
DELOACH, Thomas 37-38 Thos Sr 42
DEMAREBOIS, Marshall 39
DEMONTBOISIER, Alexandrine Marie
Julie Felicite 39
DEMSEY, W 42
DEMUEPOIS, Madame 39
DENONVILLIERS, Mr 40
DEPOLASTRON, Madame 39
DESAUSSURE, Henry W 18 22 35 37-
39 42 46 52 54 59 Henry William 1 7
20 22 39 Henry Wm 28 31-32 37 47-
50 62 64 Judge 4
DEVALL, S 1 Samuel 1
DIAMPERT, John 2
DICKINSON, Hezekiah 3
DICKS, John 8
DIGGES, Elizabeth 40 William H 40
DILLARD, Arthur 52 Philip 55 Polly 52
DOBEY, William 7
DOBY, John 6
DODGEN, William 66
DOMANICK, Agnes 64 Henry Sr 64
Marget 64
DONALDSON, David 6 Gasper 6
DONALSON, David 54
DOUGLAS, John 42 John I 41
DOWNER, Alex 3 Alexander 1-3 Alexr
1-2 14 36
DOWNEY, John 11 Mrs 11 Sally 11
DOZIER, 29 41 Ab G 54 59 Abraham
54 Abram Giles 16 Richard 51 Thos
42 William 42

DRAKE, Eason 19 Eason C 23
DRUKAM, William 18
DRURY, Moses Josiah Allen 66
DRY CREEK, 44 57
DUGLASS, John 42 Nancy 42
DUNCAN, J W 48
DUNLAP, Ann 44
DUVAL, Saml 1
DYSART, Doctor 2
EASTLAND, Jos 32
EDDINGS, Elizabeth 67 Joseph 67
EDDINS, Benjn 60 Joseph 21
EDGEFIELD, 8 10 16 23 38 43 50 67
EDGEFIELD COURT HOUSE, 20 23
32-33 50 58
EDGEFIELD COURTHOUSE, 21 60
EDGEFIELD DISTRICT, 8 14 19 25 29
48 61-62
EDGEFIELD SOUTH CAROLINA, 22
EDGEFIELD VILLAGE, 31
EDISTO, 30
EDISTO RIVER, 29
EDMONDS, A 15
EDMUNDS, A 12 32 Alexander 36
Alexr 18
EIDSON, James 42
EIGNER, Philip 42
ELDER, Mary 50
ELLIS, William 19
ELLISON, 10 15 24 28-29 Doctor 56 W
21 30 William 20-21 Wm 6 20-21 37
ENOREE RIVER, 60
ETHEREDGE, S 37
ETHERIDGE, Aaron 66
ETHRIDGE, Aaron 66
EVANS, George W 11
FAIR FOREST CREEK, 60
FARGESON, Barkley 6
FARRAR, Chesley 18 Peter 14-15 Peter
Jr 14-15 Peter Sr 14-15 Thomas 60
FARRER, Peter Jr 14
FARROW, Chaney 67 John 7 Peter 15
Peter Jr 15 Peter Sr 15 Sarah 67
FELPS, Enorah 6
FERGUSON, Barkley 4 9 Eleazar 37
Eleazer 37 John 37 John Sr 37 Mary
37 Nelson 37 Nelson F 37 Thomas
37

FERGUYSON, Thos 37
FERNANDEZ, Don Juan 36
FERREL, Ephraim 18-19 Mary 18-19
FERRELL, Ephraim 19 Mary 18-19
FINDLEY, Edward 67 John 56 Mary 67
FISH CREEK, 12
FITZSIMMONS, Christopher 23
FLEMING, John 20
FLINT, Margaret 20 Mrs 20
FLUKER, Elizabeth 65 George 65
    William 66 Wm 66
FOATS, 7
FORSYTH, William 27
FORT, Arthur 66
FORT MOORE BLUFF, 34
FOWLER, Lewis 66
FOX, James 34 John 57 N 7 Nicholas 18
FOXES CREEK, 62
FRANCE, 39-40
FRANKLIN, Isome 54
FRAZIER, Benj 51 Benjamin 51 67
    John 51 John M 51 Rebekah 51
    Sarah Adaline 51 Thomas N 51
FREEMAN, Garret 32 James 37
FUDGE, Onemus 54
FULLER, Jane 2-3 Joseph 11 18 23
    Joseph Jr 63
GAGE, George G A 18
GAILIARD, Theodore 28
GAILLARD, John 38 Theodore 1 7 20
    22 37 39
GALLMAN, Benj 5 Benjamin 4 6 9 50
    Elizabeth S 9 Mary 9 Priscilla H 9
    Rachel H 9 Sarah 9 Susan H 9
    William 50 William G 9
GALMAN, S 4
GALPHIN, George 23 Mrs 14 Thomas
    23 Thoms 20
GANES, Geo 11
GANTT, Richard 21
GARDINER, James C 34 James Cotton
    34 Mary 34
GARDNER, Barksdale 27 49 James C
    35-36 Martha 27
GARGANUS, William 21
GARNDER, 49
GARNER, Barzel 19
GARRET, Stephen 22

GARRETT, 2 Jno C 18 John 2 67
    Stephen 14-15 22 30-31 36-37 50 67
    Thomas 19 53 62 Thos 23 W 20
    William 10-11 19 33 Wm 10 31
GAYLON, Jacob 2
GEORGIA, 20 23 26 32 34 40 49 61 65
GILBREATH, Catharine 29-30 John 29
GILLESPIE, Jas 2
GILLION, Isaac 42
GLANTON, John 58
GLASCOCK, 10 21 24 29 50-51 54 J 49
    John S 6 32 48
GLOVER, Amelia 44 Archibald 44
    Benjamin 11 Charles 21 Clarissa 44
    David 44 Elizabeth 44 Elvira 21
    Frances 44 John 34 37 Martha 44
    Mary 44 Matthew 44 Portia 44
    Rebecca 21 Robert 21 44 Robert D
    21 Wiley 49 William 44
GLUKER, George 66
GOLDMAN, Benjamin 9 Mary 9 Sarah
    9
GOODE, Eliza 9-10 48 Garland 42
    Mackeness 9-10 Mackerness 48
    Mackerness P 48 Phillip 42
    Susannah 9-10
GOODMAN, Mr 20
GOODWIN, 4 7 9 31 35-36 53 Charles
    2 8 23 30 33 58 60-61 Chas 7-8 13-
    15 28 33 Chris 1 Elizabeth Eliza 23
GORAYOIT, 42
GORGRIT, Dennis 42
GOUDY, Prudence 61
GOUEDY, Mrs 31 P 31
GOWDY, James 43
GRADUEL, Robt 53
GRAVES, Geo 22 George 16 22 59 65
    Mary 16
GRAY, John 6 8 John Sr 7 53
GREEN, Ann 28 61 Bodia 28 Coclia 61
    Frances 28 61 John 19 28 42 61 Silas
    28 61 William 28 61 Willm 29
GREEN RIVER, 60
GREENE COURTHOUSE, 35
GREENVILLE, 60
GREENWOOD, William 23
GRICE, John 4 6
GRIFFIN, Joseph 54

GRIFFIS, Mrs 18

GRISSOM, William 54

GRUBS, Elizabeth P 33 Elizabeth Prior 33 Eve 33 Susanna Prior 33 Tobias P 33 Tobias Prior 33 William P 33 William Prior 33 Wm Prior 33

GRUMBLES, Benjamin 23 63 George 23

GUBS, Susanna P 33

GUNNELS CREEK, 47 57

HACKNEY, Joseph 10-12 Mrs 11 Polly 10-11

HADDON, Sarah 42 Wm 42

HAGINS, Wm 61

HALCOMBE, James 20

HALE, William 18

HALEKER, Benja 17

HALFWAY SWAMP, 9-10

HALIFAX COUNTY VIRGINIA, 10

HALL, Amy 61 Armstead 61 63 Eliza 61 James 61 John 23 28-29 53 61-63 Lucy 61 Martha Ann 61 Miles 61 63 Patcy 63 Patsy 61 Prudence 61 Richard 61 Sally 61 T 22 Thomas 61 William 19 30 61 63 Wm 30

HALLIMAN, Edmond 11

HAMILTON, Alexander Colhoun 67 Andrew 48 Delphia Adelia 67 Ransom 53

HAMMOND, Andrew Jackson 12 Ann 12 Charles 12 19 30 36-37 54 Chas 36-37 Chs 36 Col 33 Eliza 12 Frances Julia 12 J 36-37 John 30 36-37 John Jr 12 Leroy 8 12 19 22-23 30 33 60-63 Leroy Jr 12 22 Leroy Sr 12 Lewis 56 Lewis L 12 Samuel 36 60 Samuel Jr 36 Sarah Q 30 33 Sarah Quarles 12 60 Susanna 22 William 12 Wm 56

HAMPTON, Edward 18

HANCOCK, Bennet 66 George 22 62-63

HANNAH, Alexander 15 Ann 15

HARBIRT, Thos 42

HARBUCK, John 6

HARDEN, Levi 57 Margaret 29 Sarah 6 Wm 50

HARDLABOR CREEK, 32

HARDLABOR OF STEPHENS CREEK, 32

HARDY, Anna 65 Clara 61 Clarissa 28 Daniel 28 61 Elizabeth 28 Freeman 19 John 4 6 11 28 61 66 Mary 28 Polly 28 61 William 58 65-66 Wm 58

HARRIS, Benjamin 2-3 Benjn 2 Edward 40 Eliza 23 Geo 32 James A 52 Lee W 40 Lewis 34 Lud 2-3 23-24 34 Sophia 3 William 42

HARRISON, Edward 61 James 57 Mary 61

HART, Cecilia 63 Mary 63

HARTFIELD, Asa 35

HARVY, Benja 19 Thomas 7

HASTING, Benjamin 54 Elizabeth 55

HASTINGS, Benjamin 54 57 Elizabeth 54 57

HATCHER, Archibald 14 J 1 36 39 45 Jeremiah 4 9 15 33 John 29

HATTON, Joseph 52

HAWES, Isaac 37

HAWS, Isaac 11

HAY, 41

HAY'S PLANTATION, 41

HAYS, James 42 Patrick 3

HAZEL, Phillip 66

HEAD, James 68

HENNCY, John 6

HENRY, M 59

HERALD, Augusta 12

HERNDON, Mr 63 Stephen 43 63-64 Susannah 43 63 Susannh 64

HERRIN, Mary 51 Phillip 51

HERRING, Sander C 57

HIDLE, Elizabeth 47-48 John 47 Martin 47-48 Mr 48

HIGGINSON, William 23

HIGHTOWER, B 2-3 Benjamin 1 Benjamin Sr 50 Joseph 18

HILL, Abel 57-58 Elizabeth 57 Harriet 57 Harriett 57 Jesse 32 Joel 32 John 57 Lavica 57 Lodowick 37-38 Mahulda 57 Marg 57 Margaret 57 Mary 57-58 Nancy 57 Narcissa 57 Priscilla 57 Sally 57 Saml 57-58 Samuel 57-58 Sarah 57 Susan 57

HILL (cont.)
Widow 58 William 53 57 Wm 6
HIX, 14 James 12 31
HOBCAN FERRY, 38
HODGES, Mary 53
HOGANS, Ridgeway 7
HOLLADAY, Anna 30 Elenor 30 James
30-31 Lydia 30 Peggy 30 Sarah 30
William 30-31
HOLLAND, Priscilla 8 Sealy 8
HOLLIDAY, Sarah 30 William 30
William Sr 30
HOLLODAY, John Jr 66
HOLLOW CR, 8
HOLLOWAY, Anderson 30 61 Ann 30
61 Asa 46 Asas 46 Benjamin 68
Caleb 66 Douglas 25 31 46 Douglass
25 30 Edward 44 Edward B 49 Edwd
B 49 Elizabeth 30 Frances 44 Francis
44 George 30 61 James 30 John 30
61 Jordan 50-51 66 Lewis 49 Martha
30 61 68 Mary 30 44 Morris P 50
Nancy 61 Pearson 30 Pierson 31
Rachel 49 Rebecca 50 Samuel 68
Thomas 30 49 61 63 Thomas O 49
Thos 44 William 30 61 Wm 30
HOLMES, Edward 11 Fedrick 51
Frederick 51 Hodge 34 Patience 51
William 43 58
HOLSONBACK, Jacob 11 John 11
HOLT, Philip 11
HOMES, William 58
HOMES CREEK, 44
HOPKINS, Bodia 28 Coclia 61 Isaac 23
28-29 61
HORNS CREEK, 6-7 52 67
HORSE CREEK, 12 30 51
HOUSE, James 66
HOWARD, Batte 49 Enoch 64 Enos 19
Seth 19 54
HOWEL, 14 Nathaniel 8
HOWELL, Ann 2 Casper 2 Daniel 42
Hartwell 2 Nathaniel 1-2 36 Nathl 2
36
HOWL, Thos H 11
HOWLE, Thomas H 18
HUDDLESTON, Jane 5 Joseph 5
HUDLE, Wm 6

HUDSON, Isaac 42 James 42
HUGGINS, Elizabeth 47-48 Elizabeth
Hidle 48 Mark 47-48 Mrs 48
HUGH, John 53
HUGHES, 45
HUGHS, Isaac 37
HUNT, Memucan 10
HUNTER, James 1-2 Jas 3
HUTCHINS, Joseph 39
HUTTON, Genl 30 Jos 30 Joseph 29
HYDRAC, Polly 30
HYDRIGHT, Hathorn 29 Polly 29
JACKSON, S 22 Thomas 11
JAMES, John 63 W 19 William 1 20 39
William D 7 37 William Dobbins 22
William Dobin 64 Wm D 28
Zachariah 54
JANES, Joseph 29
JEMIMA, Elizabeth 38
JENKINS, John 51
JENNINGS, Caroline 12 Dickenson 12
Jane 12 John 12 Jos 31 Joseph 12
Lavica 57 Robert 11 57 William 57
JERGUSON, Wm 50
JETER, 51 J S 38 Jas J 21 Jno B 21
John 21 John S 8 16 33 44 Meredith
22 Rebecca 21 William 11 21 53-54
57 Wm 21
JINKINS, 7
JOHNS, Edwd 6
JOHNSON, Capt 17 Hugh 52 James 22
30 Jane 29 Jno 6 John 52 Margaret
29 Mary 3-4 6 9 17 Polly 17 Rd 4
Richard 4 6-7 9 17 27 Richd 3
William 67
JOHNSOTN, Richard 17
JOHNSTON, 41 Catharine 29 Hugh 29
James 29-30 James Jr 29 John 29
John J 29-30 Margaret 29 Mr 36 R
17 Richard 16 William 29
JONES, E 7 Edmund 7 Edward 6-7
Henry 8 James 19 James L 46 John
34 Mrs 4 Seaborn 2 William 24 Wm
24
JOURNAGIN, Asa 38 Jesse 38
JOUST, Abraham 18
JULIAN, Rachel 38
JULOW, John 52

KADDELL, Geo E 36
KEAN, 44
KEDDELL, Geo E 36 Geo Eveleigh 36
KELLEN, Madame 40
KEMP, Wiley 54 Wilson 51
KENNEDY, Polly 27 William 27
KENNEY, John 7
KENTUCKY, 40
KERBLAY, Jeanne L 39-40 Jeanne
    Lequino 39 Jeanne Odette Marie De
    Levis 39 Joseph Marie Lequinio 39
    Joseph Marie Lequino 39 Lequino
    39-40 Madam 40 Mr 40 Mrs 40
KERRY, John 6
KEY, Henry 43 57 John 47 Martha 43
    Tandy M 43
KIDDELL, George E 36-37 George
    Eveleigh 36
KIDDLE, George E 37 George Eveleigh
    36
KILCREASE, John 57 Minor 57 Susan
    57 Thomas 58 Thos 58
KILGORE, Jesse 2
KILLERCADE, Edmd 11
KINES FORK, 12
KING, Henry 38 William 11
KINNARD, Ro J 40
KIRKLAND, Isaac 29
KITTLE TRACT, 60
KNOP, Frederick 56
KOHNILY, Christopher 66
LABORD, Peter 31
LAFITTE, James A 40
LAIRS, Frederick 11
LAMAR, Charles 16-19 Edward 17-18
    Frances 6 James 6-7 16-18 John 11
    Polly 17 Thomas 8 Thos 41 Ths 17
LAMARS, James 17
LAMKIN, Peter 2
LANDRUM, A 7 Abner 14 John 51
LANHAM, Jonas 57
LANIER, Catherine 27 James 26 Jas 26
LARK, Andrew L 42 Andrew Lee 42
    63-64 Cullin 63 Nancy 43
LASSITTER, Abraham 56
LAWLESS, J 44
LEAF, River Mississippi 35
LEAFORD, Jane 42 Robert 42

LEAVENSWORTH, Melines C 37
    Melines Conckling 37
LEE, Andrew 43 63-64 Andw 42 63
    Gerhsam 64 Gersham 43 63-64
    Hannah 43 63-64 Jno W 64 John 64
    John W 43 63-64 Nancy 42-43 63
    Sarah 43 63-64 Susannah 43 63
    Wilson 42-43 63-64
LEIGH, Walter 1 3 40
LENOIR, John 61 Lucy 61
LEQUINIO, 40
LESLIE, Panton 36
LEVENSWORTH, Melines C 33
LEVINGSTON, Jas 12 Robert 18
LEWIS, Benj 42 Frederick 11 R C 7
    Richard 57 Wm H 38
LEXINGTON DISTRICT, 47
LICK CRREK, 45
LILLY, David 44
LINCOLN COUNTY TENNESSEE, 63
LINDSEY, Benjn 54
LIPSCOMB, John 37-38 Nathan 46
    Sarah 37-38 Sarah M 38 Sarah
    Marey 37 Sarah Mary 37-38
LITTLE, John 40-41 Saluda 41 Sarah
    40-41 William 41 Wm 42
LITTLE BEAVER DAM, 60
LITTLE EDISTO, 60
LITTLE SALUA, 38
LITTLE SALUDA, 65
LITTLE SALUDA RIVER, 37
LITTLE STEPHENS CREEK, 38
LITTLE STEPHENS CREEK
    MEETING HOUSE, 38
LITTLETON, John 56
LIVINGSTON, Elizabeth 44 John 44
    Taliaferro 43 Taliofero 24
LIVINGSTON NELSON COUNTY, 40
LIVINSWORTH, Miles 2
LOLLY, John 4
LONG, Elizabeth 45 Jacob 45
LONG CANE ABBEVILLE
    DISTRICT, 46-47
LONGMIRE, John 19 32
LONGSTREET, Gilbert 48 James 50
    Jas 50
LORRY, Elizabeth 45 Jacob 45
LOVELACE, David 57 Mary 57

LOVELESS, D M 57
LOWE, Henry W 58 John 34 Nicholas
 42
LUCAS, Abraham 54 John 53 Solomon
 28 61 Solr 20
LUNDAY, Hezekiah 47
LUNDRY, James 47 Polly 47
LUNDY, Abraham 47 Abram 47
 Hezekiah 47 John 47 Nancy 47
 Zachh 47
LYON, Elijah 32 55-56 John 32 58 62
 Polly 32
MACK, Benjamin 19
MACMURPHY, Geo Y 11
MACUS, Daniel 54
MADISON COUNTY ALABAMA, 68
MAIT, William 11
MALICHI, 38
MALONE, Elizabeth 34-35 Elizabeth A
 34 James 34-35
MANN, John H 2-3
MANNING, 42
MARBRY, Thomas 18
MARCUS, Daniel 59
MARITN, Thomas R 16
MARK, Peggy 56
MARLBOROUGH DIST, 7
MARLBOROUGH DISTRICT, 6
MARSH, Amelia 4 B 16 49 Bryan 16
 Bryant 15 Martha M 44 Mary B 60
 Milley 5-6 Millie 4 Milly 3-5 8 27
 Mrs 5 Robert 6 45 54 S 28 Saml 5-7
 9 17 28 Samuel 3-9 27 44 54 58 60
 68 Thomas 4 6 Thos 6
MARSHAL, Bailey 6
MARSILLAC, Louis Sylvester Debrugy
 39
MARSILLACE, Therese Gabrielle 39
MARTIN, 14 Abraham 43 Bartlett 22 C
 Jr 50 Charles 10-11 16 Charles Jr 54
 Charles Sr 54 David 7 Henry 11
 James 11-12 Joel 21 John 44 John A
 S 12-13 16 John Allen Scott 12 16
 65 Mary 7 Mr 32 Prudence 10-11 R
 10 Reeves 9-10 Thomas 11 Thomas
 P 12 16 54 Thos 11 Zachariah 21
MASON, George 42
MATHEWS, Drewry 27 Drury 41-42

MATHEWS (cont.)
 Elizabeth 41 John 3 Lewis 41-42
 Mourning 41
MATTHEWS, Anna 65 Budcade 65-66
 Budeade 65 Cabel 65-66 Cabell 65
 Daniel 65-66 Drury 40 66 Eleanor
 65-66 Elizabeth 40 65-66 Enoch 65-
 66 Hardy 65-66 Isaac 65 James 36
 Josiah Allen 66 Lewis 40 65-66
 Mark 25-26 Martha 65-66 Mary 65
 Mary Quarles 66 Micajah 65-66
 Milberry 66 Moses 65-66 Moses
 Mathis 65 Mourning 40 Nancy 66
 William 65-66
MAUBOIR, Jeanne Odette Marie De
 Levis 39
MAUBOIX, 39
MAULDIN, Caleb 42
MAXZEY, Dr 9
MAY, Edmund 66
MAYS, Anna 67 Gardner 66 Joseph 66
 Mathew 21 53 Matthew 66 S 14
 Saml 42 Stephen 54 W 7 William
 66-67 William B 67-68
MAYSON, Charles 43 Charles C 48
 Chas 31 John 44 John C 43-44 Willis
 43
MAZAKE, D 37
MAZYCK, Benjamin 50 Daniel 60
 William 60
MAZYCK TRACT, 60
MCCOY, Archd 2 Archibald 2
MCCRACKAN, J 16
MCDOWALL, P 42
MCDUFFIE, 2 7 9 13 15-17 21 25 27
 29-30 38 49-50 52 58 G 31
MCFARLAND, A 42
MCFARLANE, A 42
MCGILLVERY, Martha 2
MCGILVERY, Martha 2
MCHAN, Mark 15
MCHOWE, Mark 39
MCKEE, Daniel 22
MCKENZIE, 59
MCKIE, Charles 11 Daniel 47 49 Mr 18
 Nancy 47 Thomas 17 Thos 17 49
 Tom 16-18
MCKINNEY, Barna 23

MCKOY, Archd 2
MCLANE, Mark 15
MCMCQUEEN, Ann 22
MCMILLAN, Bennett 30 Lydia 30
MCMURDY, Robert 2
MCMURPHY, G Y 12 George Y 10-12
   K P 11 Kesiah 11 Kesiah P 11-12
   Mrs 11
MCQEEN, James 63
MCQUEEN, Ann 22 62 Caroline 22 62
   James 22-23 37 62-63 Peter 22 62
   William 22 62 William Henry 62
MCRAE, John 35
MCREA, Robert 27
MCROWE, Daniel 49 Sarah 49
MEALING, Henry 44
MELTON, William 26
MERIWETHER, Thomas 22 Thos 22
   59
MEYER, Jonathan 2
MEYERS, David 8 Jno 14 Mrs 20
MICHLER TRACT, 52
MICOU, W 3 William 1 Wm 3
MIDDLETON, Agatha 67 Delphia
   Adelia 67 Elisabeth 65 Elizabeth 16
   64 67 Hugh 67 Hugh Jr 67 John 16
   22 59 64-65 67 Lucy 67 Mary 67
   Milly 67 Patsey 67 Sally 67 Thomas
   38 William 67
MIDDLTON, John 65
MILLER, Anna B 59-60 Elizabeth 12
   George 8 59-60 James 17 60 John 1
   23 49 Nathan 34
MILLS, 12 T 13 T S 36 Thomas 13
   Thomas S 35 Thos J 36 Thos S 36
MIMS, Briton 3 Cinthia 59 David 12-13
   16 58-59 65 M 6-7 22 37 Matt 59
   Matthew 33 Sarah 16 65
MINE, 41
MINOR, Jerry 20 William 1
MINORS BRIDGE, 8
MINTER, Ebenezer 43 Elizabeth 43
   James 43 John 43 Mackerness 11
   Mcness 43 Rebecca 43 William 43
MISSISSIPPI, State 35
MISSISSIPPI TERRITORY, 10 40
MITCHEL, Charles 54 Clarissa 44
   Edwd 54 Hinchey 54 John 50

MITCHEL (cont.)
   Samuel 44 Sion 45 Starling 6
MITCHELL, Clarissa 44 Hinchall 58
   Hinchell 58 Hinchwill 58 John 5
   Rachel 67 Saml 44 Starling 4 67
MOBLEY, James 42 John 37-38
MONDAY, James 57
MOON, Meredith William 63 Meredith
   Wm 42 N W 63 Nancy 63 William
   Meredith 64
MOORE, Anderson 50 David 19
   Elizabeth 9 50 George B 9 J 14 59
   John 11 44 49-50 John Elder 9
   Jonathan 18 Mary 50 Mary Ann 50-
   51 Mary Graves 65 Rebecca 50
   Right N 50-51 Sarah 9 Will 42
   William 50 William Anderson 50
MORAND, Catharine Agnes De Levis
   Chateau 39
MORGAN, Abiah 11 Eli 6 44 Elias 27
   Francis 44 J 47 James 44 John 27
   Lucinda 44 Lucy 27 Margaret 27
   Martha 27 Nancy 27 Polly 27 Portia
   44 William 27
MORGAN COUNTY GEORGIA, 6
MORRIS, Ann E 60 John 56
MORRISS, Thomas 66
MOSELEY, Alex 56 Hugh 56
MOSLEY, James 29
MOSS, P 10
MOUNT ENON GEORGIA, 32
MOUNTAIN CREEK, 50
MUEBROS, Guy Casimer Adelaide De
   Levis 39
MUEPOIS, Charles Chibut Marie
   Gaston De Levis 39
MUIBOIS, Catharine Agnes De Levis
   Chateau 39 Louis Marie Francois
   Gaston De Levis 39
MUNSON, Lemuel 49-50
MURRAY, John 34
MURREY, John 54
MUSTERFIELD BRANCH, 8
MYER, Johnathan 34 Jonathan 14
MYERS, Jonathan 13
NAIL, Caspar 2 Casper 1 14-15 Casper
   Sr 8 14 Daniel 13 Gasper 13 15 34
   Jona 42

NAILE, Daniel 13 Gasper 13
NASH, E 41 Ezekiel 41-42
NAYLE, A G 7
NEAL, Casper 15-16 Gasper 36 Mr 16
    20 Mrs Daniel 20
NEALE, Gasper Sr 35
NEALS, 16
NEGEO, Aimy 28
NEGRO, Abbe 48 Abbey 2-3 Abraham
    48 Abram 22 54 Adam 23 Aggy 21
    68 Aimy 27 Alfred 6 28 Altama 6 27
    Altamont 7 28 Amy 4 6 16 58
    Andrew 11 16 Anney 23 Anniky 10
    Anthony 65 Armstead 65 Barbra 49
    Beck 22 28 Becky 6 Beiner 22 Ben 4
    6 55-56 Benjamin 9 28 Biners 22
    Boatswain 3 Bob 6 11 17 21 42 65
    Cate 4 55 Cato 4 6 9 28 Caty 28
    Ceiley 21 Celiny 9 Charity 9
    Charles 3-4 6 17 28 54 Charlotte 11
    Chloe 41-42 Clara 4 Clarinda 23
    Clary 6 Cloey 16 Colyet 7 Connetta
    4 Curry 16 22 Cyrus 11 Dave 6-7
    David 4 27-28 Davy 11 Delcey 11
    Derry 7 Dick 3 11 22 34-35 Dilsey
    50 Dina 3 Dinah 65 Doll 34-35 41-
    42 Dorcas 23 Duomony 3 Eady 49
    Edy 11 22 Eliza 21-22 Emly 42
    Ephraim 55 Ester 42 Fan 55-56
    Fanney 50 Fanny 23 56 Frank 42
    Friday 11 Gabe 11 George 11 21 55-
    56 Gibb 4 28 Glasgow 23 Green 6
    Greenberry 27 Hal 58 Hall 16 54
    Hannah 4 6-7 9 27 41-42 68 Harriet
    4 7 27 49 Harriett 6 28 Harry 3 10 21
    Henry 6 27 Isaac 4 6 21 24-26 28 37
    48 Isaack 11 Jack 3-4 6 11 28 34-35
    48 Jacob 34-35 James 22 27 49 Jane
    35 42 Jas 4 Jean 29 Jeaney 49 Jeffery
    34 Jeffry 35 Jemima 2 Jenney 65
    Jenny 13 16 34 Jere 4 Jerry 6-7 Jim
    14 34-35 49 Jimmy 3 Joe 23 49 John
    28 Joicy 49 Juda 26 Judah 49 Jude
    21 24-25 Judy 3 16 58 Julius 42 Kate
    6 15 54 Let 48 Lett 48 Lewis 17 41-
    42 Lise 55 Little Cargie 17 Little
    Ned 6-7 London 14 Lonijo 6
    Lorenzo 28 Lowden 31

NEGRO (cont.)
    Lucy 27-28 34-35 49-50 Lyd 42
    Lydia 41 Mabl 3 Mahala 6 27
    Mahaly 28 Mall 3 Margaret 28 Maria
    6 21 Mariah 11 Mary 4 6 21 28
    Milley 6 Milly 4 7 9 27 Minte 11
    Morress 42 Morris 49 Moses 6 27-28
    Mossess 42 Mourning 10 Nan 29
    Nance 27 42 Nancy 11 21 24 49 65
    Ned 4 7 9 11 Nel 16 Nell 13 Nero 6
    28 Nothward Dick 16 Offy 42 Old
    Dick 16 Old Ned 6-7 Old Tom 11
    Paddy 37 Pat 11 Pegg 23 Peter 4 6
    13 16 21-22 28 41-42 65 68 Phebe
    11 Polashy 9 Polaski 7 27 Poll 54
    Pompey 11 Prince 11 Pulaski 4
    Quomoni 3 Rachel 4 6-7 9 14 20
    Rhoda 49 Rhody 49 Richard 6
    Robbin 11 Rodger 3 Rody 49 Rose 3
    Sally 3 6 23 Sam 11 16 28 54-55 64-
    65 Sammy 55 Sarah 28 49 54 Sary
    42 Scipio 35 Scippio 34 Sealy 68
    Sela 35 Selah 34 Shepherd 4 6 Silla
    49 Silver 50 Silvey 27 Silvia 7 64
    Silvy 4 6 Simon 68 Sina 41-42
    Spencer 21 Stephen 23 55 Sue 3 6-7
    27-28 Sylias 37 Tabby 10 Talitha 42
    Terry 22 Thursa 6 27-28 Tom 11 27
    64 Toney 11 50 Tony 41-42 Tresa 22
    Viney 49 Violet 49 Will 2-3 22 28
    65 William 6 Windsor 15 Winney
    41-42 Yellow Will 9 Young Ned 4
    Zack 22
NEILSON, John 20
NELSON, William 56 Wm 56
NELSON COUNTY VIRGINIA, 40
NESBIT, Allen 8
NESBITT, Agnes 20 Allen 19-20 Hugh
    20
NESITT, Hugh 20
NEW, Daniel 11
NEW RICHMOND, 12
NEW WINDSOR TWP, 3
NEW WINDSOR TWP GRANVILLE
    COUNTY, 2
NEWBERRY DISTRICT, 63
NEWBEY, James 37
NEWBY, James 37

NEWMAN, John 19-20 Lucy 27 Nancy
    Ann Crawford 27 Priscilla 8 R 9
    Reuben 27 Richard 5 8-9
NEWPORT, Robert 42
NEWSOM, William 11
NIBBS, William 33
NICHOLS, Elizabeth 28 George 54
    William 28-29 61 Willm 29 Wm 20
    28
NICHOLSON, Irbin 52 Wright 42
NICOLSON, Wm 42
NIELSON, John 64-65
NIELY, William 14
NINETY SIX DIST, 11
NINETY SIX DISTRICT, 45 65
NISBET, Hugh 20
NIX, Charles 43
NIXON, H A 11 56
NOBLE, Patrick 46
NOBLES, Hezekiah 57 Mrs 6 William 6
NOLAND, Benjamin 2
NORRIS, Joseph 56 Nathan 45 Stephen
    18
NORTON, John 56
NORWOOD, Nathl 63
NUMAN, Mrs 6
O'HARA, Cynthia 52 James 52
O'HARRAH, Charles 52
O'NEAL, Charles 52 Charlotte 52
O'NEALL, Charles 52
ODOM, A 5 Abraham 5 9 Abraham Jr 5
    Abram 6 Benjamin 6 Celia 5 7 Jacob
    5 John P 6 Lewis 5 7 Mary 5 Nancy
    5 Willis 5
ODONAL, Elezer 57
ODUM, Abraham 5 8 Benjamin 8 Jacob
    8 Jancy 8 Jane 8-9 John 7 Lewis 8
    Mary 8 Michael 8 Milly 8 Nancy 8
    Sally 8 Sealy 8 Vicey 8 Willis 8-9
OGLESBY, Thomas 43
OHARA, Cynthia 53 J 59 James 53
OHARRA, Cynthia 59 James 59 Jas 59
    Mrs 53
OHARROW, Cynthia 59 James 59
OLD, Charles 18
OLDS, Charles 22 William W 64-65
    Wm 64 Wm W 65
OLIPHANT, 14 Jno 14

OWENS, Enoch 37
OWENSBY, James 11
OZBORNE, Ross 38
PACE, Cabell 65 Thomas 65
PACOLET RIVER, 39
PALMER, Dabney 51
PANTON, James 19-20
PARDIEU, Sarah 3
PARDUE, 29 F 37
PARIS, 40
PARISH, 5
PARKER, 1 Daniel 54 Elizabeth 50 58
    Geo 7 50 58 Isaac 8 50 Jas 6 John 52
    Samuel 58 Wm 2
PARKINS, Danl 42
PARNALL, John 42
PARTAIN, Ezekil 42 Ezekl 42 William
    26
PARTLOW, John 42
PASERY, Catharine 34
PATRIC, Ninian 3
PATRICK, George Lewis 64 Hannah 43
    63-64 Lewelling 64 Lewis 43 63-64
PAVNY, Catherine 35
PEARSON, Aaron 7
PENDLETON DISTRICT, 26
PENDLETON ORANGEBURG
    DISTRICT, 60
PERRIN, Robert 56 Samuel 10
PERRY, Benjn 56 Crawford 52
PERRYMAN, Mumford 37-38 42
PETERS POINT BARNWELL, 60
PETERSON, John G 52
PHELPS, Enoch 7
PHILIPS, Elbert 2 Jonathan 2
PICKETS, James 12
PICKETT, James 11
PIERCE, Reuben 11
PINCKNEY, Thos 6
PINEY WOODS HOUSE, 21
PINKNEY, Charles C 42
POINSETT, J R 24
POINTSETT, J R 23 R 24
POLLEY, 14
POND, William 63
PONDS, Mary 50 William 50
PONPON RIVER, 38
PONTNIGHT, 47

POOL, John 10 Mitchell 61
POOLE, Elizabeth 61 63 John 9
POOLS MUSTER, 10
POPE, Charity 41 Elizabeth 40-41 65
    Ezekiel 41 Henry 41 Jacob 65-66
    John 40-42 Mary 40-41 Mourning
    40-41 Patience 41 Sampson 41-42 52
    66 Solomon 40-42 Solomon L 41
    Solomon Lewis 40 Solomon Sr 41-
    42 Susannah 41 Temperance 41
    Wiley 41-42
POPLE, Solomon 41
POSEY, Francis 42
POSTELL, Benjamin 38
POTTER, 37
POTTS, Daniel 42
POWEL, 45 William 54
POWER, John 27
PRENTIS, James O 34 James Olid 8
    James Olis 8 James Otis 33
PRESCOTT, Moses 60
PRICE, Ambrose 11 William 11 32 56
    William Jr 32 Wyley 11
PRINCE, Edward 22
PRIOR, Elizabeth 34 Jno 1 John 1-2 8
    33 60-61 John Jr 33 Mary 8 Morlow
    L 3 Sarah 8 33 Tobias 8 William 33
    Wm 33
PRYOR, J 14 John 2 14
PURDUE, 30
PURSELL, Wm 49
QUARLES, Cabel Mary 66 David 18
    Francis 47 Francy 46 Hughy 46-47
    James 18-19 32 Jas 18 John 46
    Richard 18-19 46 67 Richd 32 Sally
    67 Saml 6 Samuel 19 46-47 Sarah 46
    William 18-19 46 Wm 18
RABB, James 42 Patience 40 42
RABORN, Joseph 26
RABURN, Joseph 25
RADCLIFF, Richard 31
RAMBO, Albert 50 Albert Jefferson 22
    50 62 Augusta Bardwin 62 Augustus
    50 Augustus Baldwin 22 Hammond
    62 James 50 62 Jos 50 Joseph 22 62-
    63 Martha 50 Martha S 62 Martha
    Scantlin 22 Mary 50 Mary Moore 22
    62 Matilda 50

RAMBO (cont.)
    Matilda Elizabeth 22 50 62 Mrs 23
    63 Reuben 50 62 Reuben James 22
    Susanna 22-23 62 Susannah Chany
    50
RAMSAY, Charles 33-34 David 23 36
    Ephraim 23-24 34 42 John 24 30-31
    48 Judge 19 Mary Ann 23-24 Mrs 19
RAMSEY, Charles 8
RANDALL, George 28 Phoebe 28
RANDOL, George 29
RANDOLPH, Charles 54 George 28
    Isaac 6 19 54 Phoebe 28 Stephen 2
RAPLEY, Richard Andrew 20 Richd 11
RARDEN, Levin 6
RATCLIFF, 31
RAWLINS, William 10
RAYLEIGH, Abraham 66
REARDEN, Eleanor 51 Emeline 51
    Joseph 52 Nancy 52 Timothy 51
    William 51 Wm 51
RED BANK CREEK, 37-38 51
REESE, James 49
REID, Dr 7 Jas 33 R 6-7 Robert
    Raymond 2
RENNOLDS, Fielding 50
RENOLDS, Fielden 50
REYNOLDS, Fielding 50 James 7
RICHARDS, James 1-2 14 Mary 1
RICHARDSON, Abraham 29-30 David
    38 47 51 Thomas 42
RICHMOND, 40
RICHMOND COUNTY, 3
RICHMOND COUNTY GEORGIA, 1-
    2
RICHRDSON, David 37
RIDDLE, Catherine 49 Eleanor 48
    James 48 Jesse 48 John G 48 Martha
    49 Mary 49 Sarah 49 Thomas 49
    William 48 Wm 49
RIED, Joseph C 54
RIVER, Savannah 2
RIVERS, Mrs 15
ROBB, James 40-41 Patience 40-41
ROBERTS, George 42 John 42 William
    42
ROBERTSON, Mr 36 Will 2 William
    11 67

ROBINSON, Allen 22 Andrew 22 John
7
ROBUCK, Ezekiel 29 54 Polly 29
ROCKEY CREEK, 60
ROCKY CREEK, 60
RODGERS, Collin 14
ROEBUCK, Ann 28 Benjamin 28 61
Black 28 Clarissa 28 Elizabeth 28
Ezekiel 28 61 James 28 61 John 28-
29 61 Mary 28 Phoebe 28 Polly 28
61 Robert 28-29 Winifred 28
Winney 28
ROEBUCKS, Ezekiel 12
ROGERS, Catherine 57 Daniel 66
Gazaway 57 Thomas 1-2
ROLLEY, Reason 45
ROPER, Benj 18 Charles 19 David 19
David Sr 19 John 18
ROSE, Hu 60 Martin 11
ROSS, John 66
ROWE, Daniel M 49 Sarah 49
ROWELL, Edward 33
ROWLAND, Nathan 42
ROZEN, R 37
RUDISILL, John 54
RUDSILL, John 54
RUNNELL, Benj 6
RUNNELS, Fielding 50 54
RUNNOLS, John 54
RUNOLS, James 54
RUSSEAU, James 3
RUSSEL, Thos C 37
RYAN, Amelia 4 27 Ben 7 Benj 3 5-7
27 Benjamin 4-9 27-28 Benjamin
Jabez 9 Benjamin Jr 9 Benjamin Sr
4-6 9 27 Benjn 6 28 Emilia 6 Emillia
6 Jno 5 John 3-6 9 27-28 53 68 John
E 6 John Sr 4 6 Lacon 6 9 Margaret 9
Milly 8-9 27 Mrs 5 Pickens E 9
Sampson 9 Sarah 9 Stanmore B 9
William C 9
RYON, John 6 Martha 6
SADDLER, Isaac 66
SAINT BARTHOLOMEW PARISH,
38
SAINT JAMES PARISH SANTEE
CRAVEN COUNTY, 38
SALTER, John 41-42

SALUDA, River 9
SALUDA RIVER, 42 45 52 60 63
SAMSON, John Francis 61
SAMUEL, Amelia 44 Beverly 33 49-50
Museo 44 Robert 7 Wm 50
SANDERS, Ambrose 42
SANDFORD, Frederick 3 William 3
SANDIFER, 58
SANTEE, 38
SARZEAU MORBIHAN, 40
SAVAGE, John 14 S 67 Samuel 67
SAVANNAH, 1 19-20 22 33
SAVANNAH RIVER, 2 8 12 22-23 40
44 58 62
SAVIZALE MORBIHAN, 40
SAWYERS, George 7 Sarah 45 William
45 William E 45
SCALES, William 54
SCANTLING, Martha 50
SCARBOROUGH, Thos 11
SCHAFFER, Mrs 20
SCOTT, Elisabeth 65 Elizabeth 16 58-
59 James 51 Jas 6 Jery 6 John 16 58-
59 65 Mary 16 58-59 65 Moses 6
Samuel 12-13 16 58-59 64-65
Samuel C 12 16 58 Samuel G 65
Samuel Sr 12 Sarah 16 Thomas 51
Will 42
SCURRY, Thomas 66 William 66
SEAFORD, Robert 42
SEARLE, John 11
SEARLES, Cavington 11
SELPHT, Daniel 56
SHACKELFORD, James 43
SHAFFER, Mary 20
SHANKLIN, Harriet 49 Saml 50 Saml
T 49
SHANNON, Saml 11 29 Samuel 29
Wm 56
SHARPTON, Jeff 15 Jeffry 22 Jephrey
22
SHAW, Christopher 53 W 37 Wm 44
SHEETZ, 45
SHELNUT, Geo 31
SHEPPARD, Thomas 47
SHINHOLSER, 14
SHINHOLSTER, 1 Mrs 20 William 1-2
34

SHUG, Phillip 66
SIDY, Martha 39
SIGLER, Jeremiah 43
SILVER BLUFF, 8 23
SIMKINS, 2 9 15 17 21 30-31 38 50 52
 58 Arthur 36 Eldred 6-7 49 Jn 7 65
 Jno 1 13 16 18 27 54 68 John 11 14
 19 25 27 29 41 54 64 M 14 22
SIMPSON, M 11 Thos P 11
SLAPPY, Frederic 52
SLATER, George 54
SLAVE, Allick 60 Amy 60 Augustus 60
 Beason 60 Berry 60 Big Corydoin 60
 Big Jim 60 Butler 60 Cloe 60 Coclia
 60 Cupid 60 Dido 60 Esther 60
 Hannah 60 Harriet 60 Issac 60 Jane
 60 Joe 60 Jude 63 Little Hannah 60
 Little Jim 60 Little Sue 60 Loudoun
 60 Molly 60 Moses 60 Muster 60
 Nance 19 Nero 60 Phillis 63
 Polydore 60 Poor Boy 60 Primis 60
 Prince 60 Pussey 60 Sally 60 Sam 60
 Silla 60 Stephen 60 Sue 60 Topaz 60
 Will 60
SLUICE, Bull 22
SMILEY, James 38
SMITH, Henry 42 Jacob 63-64 John E
 14 Luke 64 Matilda 43 Mr 63 Peter
 37 Peter Sr 37 Roger 57 Sarah 63-64
 Simeon 38 Spencer 50 William 6
 Wm 6 Zachary 19
SMYLEY, James 39
SMYLY, James 38 Samuel 38
SNEAD, Garlan 54 Mary 39 63
SNEED, A 59 Mrs 59 N 59
SOUTH CAROLINA, 36
SOUTH EDISTO RIVER, 29
SPANISH TERRITORY, 1
SPARTANBURG DISTRICT, 60
SPARTANBURGH DISTRICT, 39
SPEAR, Moses 54
SPEARMAN, Edward 52 Susannah 52
SPEARS, Moses 54
SPENCE, Doctor 38
SPICER, Patrick 37
SPRAGINS, Wm 64
SPRATT, Alexander 39 Elizabeth 39
 James 39 John 39 Mandy 39

SPRATT (cont.)
 Margaret 39 Martha 39 Mary 39
 Rachel 39 Sally 39 Thomas 39
ST AUGUSTINE E F, 36
STALLWORTH, Joseph 52
STALNAKER, James 51 Patsey 51
STANTON, John 65 Joseph B 65
 William 64-65 Wm 64-65
STAR, John 2-3 8 60-61
STARK, 47 Robert 6
STARR, John 33
STEDHAM, John 51
STENTS, 45
STEPHENS CREEK, 31-32 57-58
STEPHENSON, Thomas 57
STEVENS, Silvanus 60
STEWART, Alexander 12 William 8 34
STILY, Jno 42
STOKES, William 10
STONE, Henry 56
STOTT, Jacob 5
STOVALL, Charles 31 Lucy 31
STROTHER, Charlotte 38 47 David 38
 47 George 38 47 George F 38
 George M 47 John 41-42
 Temperance 41 William 38 47 Wm
 38
STRUM, Henry 54
STURZENEGGER, 16 Charlotte 13 20
 Elizabeth 14 Jno 1 20 John 1-2 8 12
 14-15 31 35-36 Mrs 13 20
SULLIVAN, George 56 John 49
SUMMERS, William 9
SUMPTER DISTRICT, 61
SWARENGIN, 29 Thos 29
SWEARENGEN, Fed 17 John 17
SWEARINGHAM, Josiah 51 Mary 51
 Patsey 51 Rice 51 Van Edward 51
SWICARD, 47
TALBERD, John 10
TALBERT, Anselm 11 John 11-12
TALBOT, John 11
TALLY, Elizabeth 57 Thomas 57
TARANTS, Martin 47
TARRANCE, John 1-3 23
TAYLOE, William F 54
TAYLOR, Agnes Ann 19 Ann 13 19-20
 Anne 19 David 19 James 20

TAYLOR (cont.)
John 20 34 Martha 19 Polly 7
Reuben 66 Susanna 20 Susannah 20
Walter 2 12-14 19-20 34 Wyatt 18
TEASDALE, Isaac 36-37 Mr 37
TENNANT, Wm 18
TENNENT, Patsey 67 William 67
TERRY, J 57 John Sr 50-51 Joseph M
45 Sarah 45 William 45
THOMAS, Elisabeth 22 Elizabeth 21-22
Henry 37 James 21-22 37 58 John
21-22 John C 22 Joice 21-22
Nicholas 42 Ralph 37 Sarah 22 Silas
21-22 Stephen 43 Widow 58 William
21-22
THOMPSON, Buckner 26 David B 24
David T 25 David W 24-26 Elizabeth
66 James 3 66 Judge 24 Polly 24-25
W 7-8 14 26 32 43 48 50 56 58 60-
61 65 68 Waddy 1 7 20
THOMS, Sarah 21
THOMSON, Peter 27 Waddy 22 39
THORN, Amy 20 C 20 Ch 20
THURMOND, John 57 Pleasant 32 46-
47
TILLMAN, Benjamin 50 Benjn 49
David 54 Federick 54 Fredk 21
Maryelda 49 S 59 Stephen 6 Stephen
Jr 21 Thos 53
TIMMERMAN, John 56
TINSLEY, Arthur 25 Catharine 25
TOBIN, Cornelius 29
TOBLER, Adeline 15 Ann 15 J J 16
John J 1 15 John Joachim 15 William
15-16 Wm 14-16
TOBLERS, Wm 16
TOLBERT, 16
TOMKINS, James 57 Mahulda 57
Stephen 43
TORRENCE, John 63
TOWLS, John 66 Manrisig 66
TOWN CREEK, 8 31 33 60
TOWNSEND, Elizabeth 52 Nathaniel
52
TRAYLOR, John 65 Thomas 54
TURKENET, Henry 2
TURKEY CREEK, 51
TURPIN, Anderson 32 Mr 32

TUTT, Benj 18 James 56 Mr 14 R 46
Rd 33 Richard 19 Richd 1
TWIGGS, Abraham 20
UNION DISTRICT, 60
VALLEY OF HOPE, 58
VAUGHAN, Robert 2
VAUGHN, 63 Drewry T 64 Drury T 64
James 38 64
VIRGINIA, 10 40 49 61
VOLATON, Francis 14
WADE, Abraham 10 Abraham Marshal
10 Abraham Martin 10 Abram
Marshall 10 Anne 10 Betsy 10 Betsy
Marshal 10 Charles 10 Drayton 17 E
W 10 17 Edward 10 16-17 Edward
W 10 17-18 Edward Washington 10
16 Edwd W 17 Johnson R 17 Letty
10 Marshall 10 Martin 17 Mary 17
Sarah 16-17 Sarah B 17 Washington
10 William 10 Wm 10
WAGES, Benjn 42
WAIT, Nancy 66 Thomas 66
WAITES, Thos 28
WAITS, Elizabeth 66 Thomas 66
WALENCE, Joseph 52
WALKER, Anna 67-68 Eliza 23 Francis
33 Geo 33 George 33 James S 1 John
23 32-33 Joseph R 32 Martha J 67-
68 Mary Ann 23 Peggy 55 Rober 32
Robert 46 55 Saml 6 21 68 Samuel
58 67-68 Samuel Jr 58 Samuel Sr 67
Sarah 67-68 Silvanus 42
WALL, Amy 61 John 52 61 Wm 52
WALLACE, Joseph 32
WALLOW, George 34
WALLPOOL, Thomas 54
WALLS, William 54
WALTON, F G 48 George 2
WALTON COUNTY GEORGIA, 6
WARDLAW, Jas 20
WARREN, Elijah 42
WASH, William 54
WASHINGTON DISTRICT, 24
WATERS, Thomas 20
WATIES, Thomas 1 7 39 64
WATKINS, Anderson 20
WATSON, Aaron 54 William 19
WEAVER, Henry 66

WEBSTER, Thos 49
WELBORN, Champion 56 Wm 56
WELCH, James 34
WELLBORN, Jeremiah 15
WELLS, John 19
WEST, James 53 William 65
WHATLEY, E 53 Shurley 58 Willis 19
  Wilson 6
WHATLY, Shurly Jr 18
WHITAKER, William 65
WHITE, Fred 51 Frederick 51 Nathan
  21 Tom 20
WHITLEY, Anna 66 Elizabeth 66 John
  66 John Sr 66 Lewis 66 Stephen 66
  William 66
WHITTEN, Elisha 11
WICKES, Isaac 36
WIDEMAN, Jacob 56
WIL---, Polly 18
WILBORN, Jeremiah 14-15 Richard 43
WILBOURN, Samuel 15
WILEY, 41
WILKES COUNTY GEORGIA, 64-65
WILKISON COUNTY MISSISSIPPI
  TERRITORY, 22
WILLBORN, 15 Jeremiah 14 Pamelia
  43 Richard 43
WILLIAMS, Butler 18 53 Davis 55
  Elihu 20 Frederick 42 James 5 42-44
  60 James A 44 James Atwood 43
  Jane 5 8 John 45-46 66 Joice 22
  Joseph 48 Lucy 67 Martha 5 Martha
  Odom 5 Mary 5 8 Matilda 43 Mrs 5
  20 Nelley 48 Patty 5 8 Rebecca 43-
  44 Rebekah 44 S 32 Saml 49
  Sampson 5 Samuel 32 55 Steven 51
  Theo 5 Theophilus 5 8 Thomas 22 V
  P 54 William 2 43-44 Wm 43
WILLIAMSON, David 29 Dr 14
WILLISSON, T T 9 Thos F 37 Thos T 9
WILLS, Edger 42 John 19
WILLSON, John 35 Margaret 35
WILSON, Daniel 42 Elizabeth P 33
  Jeremiah 66 Margaret 35 Sampson
  66 Stephen 8 33 Steven 33
WINCHESTER, 40
WINHAM, John 14

WINN, Richard 61 63 Sally 61 Thos 20
WISE, 29 Capt 30
WISES CREEK, 29-30
WITHERINGTON, Richard 19
WITLOW, John 35
WITT, Martin 47-48
WOLFINGER, Leslie 13
WOLLEY, Elizabeth 45
WOOD, Joseph 34
WOODROOF, Wilson 63
WOODS, Edmond 19 James 40
  Nicholas 19
WOOLEY, Andrew 45 David 45
  Reason 45 Zacheus 45
WOOLLEY, Andrew 45 David 45
  Elizabeth 45 Nancy 45 Reason 45
  Sarah 45 Vardry 45 Zachariah 45
  Zacheus 45
WOOLLY, Andy 45 David 45 Nancy 45
  Reason 45 Vardy 45
WOOLY, Nancy 45 Vardy 45 Zacheus
  45
WRAY, Edmund 66 James 66 Matthew
  66
WREN, William 46 Wm 46
WRENN, Andrew 45-46 William 45
  Wm 46
WRIGHT, Elizabeth 18 John 19
YANCEY, 20
YELDALE, Robert 56
YOUNG, Abraham 45 Abram 46
  Charlotte 46 Jacob 45-46 Jonathan
  45-46 Laml 14 Lemuel 2 Mary 45
  Valentine 45-46
YOUNGBLOOD, Andrew 45-46 Louis
  49 Mary 49
ZAH, Brooks 52
ZINN, Agnes 34 Catharine 34 Elizabeth
  34-36 Elizabeth A 34 Henry 3 34-36
  Jacob 1-3 8 33-35 Jacob Jr 1-2 8
  Jacob Sr 33 35-36 Margaret 34 Mary
  1-3 34 Sarah 34-35 V 36 Val 36
  Valentine 34-36
ZUBLEY, Ann 13 Charlotte 13 Eleanor
  13 Mary 13 Mrs 13 Sarah 13
ZUBLY, Ann 13-14 19 34 Charlotte 20
  David 8 Mary 13 Polly 19 Sarah 13

Other Heritage Books by Carol Wells:

www.ingramcontent.com/pod-product-compliance
Lightning Source LLC
LaVergne TN
LVHW021541080426
835509LV00019B/2778